The Women Speak:

SHARED WISDOM

FOR

WOMEN MARRIED

TO

PASTORS

Wanda Taylor-Smith

This stellar book is a must read for anyone who is or knows a pastor's wife! I wish I could've read it thirty years ago as a young minister's wife. Wanda's deep insights bring clarity, compassion and keen understanding right where they are needed. This book is powerful – on a personal level for sure…and for our church families as well.

Cindy Landham
Pastor's wife,
Licensed and certified wellness coach,
Author of The Liberated Eater, *workshop leader*
Jacksonville, Florida

Dr. Wanda Taylor-Smith has brought to this narrative keen insight, a caring heart, professional skills as a nurse, and the weight of over twenty years of her own experience as a clergy wife. Through her research and numerous interactions with clergy wives, she has tapped the heart-beat of women who are married to pastors and has given voice to their inner concerns and struggles regarding their role expectation and self-image. This writer has significantly documented the attitudes, strivings, and hopes of a group of women – African American clergy wives – whose voices are usually silent and not often studied or identified in scholarly literature.

Gwendolyn Inez Massey
Clergy wife, married for 61 years,
Mental Health Counselor
Greensboro, Alabama

Dr. Wanda Taylor-Smith has heard the voices of the multitude in ministry and those who are affected by them. As a skilled and compassionate spiritual physician she gives a biblical prescription for holistic healing and preventive care. *The Women Speak* equips women entering into ministry with their husbands; empowers them in their ministry and enlightens them as they emphasize the unity that must exist in the Body of Christ.

Sheila Bailey
Widow of a pastor, Dr. E. K. Bailey,
Author and speaker,
Founder of Sheila B. Ministries
Dallas, Texas

How I wish a book like this could have been written when my husband Dick and I were called into the ministry forty years ago! I longed for encouragement and wisdom from pastors' wives on the struggles and issues of their roles. I met Dr. Wanda Taylor-Smith at one of the Pastor's Schools at Beeson Divinity School where she was leading a group of women. We met again when she came to First Presbyterian Church of Baton Rouge with her husband Dr. Robert Smith, Jr. for a preaching conference and once again Wanda opened herself up to help the wives of pastors.

I enthusiastically endorse this book. I am sure it will be an excellent resource due to her study of scriptures, her faithfulness in prayer, obedience to her Lord, and her life experience of being the wife of a pastor.

Judie Gates
Pastor's wife, married for 50 years
Baton Rouge, Louisiana

For my mate,

Dr. Robert Smith, Jr.

and

in memory of my mother,

Mrs. Martha Qualls Mason,

who set an example of being a strong woman of purpose

and

my mentor,

Mrs. Willa Marshall,

a woman who was married to a pastor

Contents

Foreword

*I*n her book *The Women Speak: Shared Wisdom from Women Married to Pastors*, Dr. Wanda Taylor-Smith writes, "Women are unique beings created as such by God, neither by mistake nor as an afterthought but by intention."

I agree.

I have known and admired Dr. Wanda Taylor-Smith for many years. I have watched her perform brilliantly in her many roles as student, nurse, mother, pastor's wife, seminary professor's wife, author, speaker, encourager, and ministry leader. She has inspired me as well as numerous other wives whose husbands work in the vocation of God's ministry. In this well-researched and very readable volume, Dr. Taylor-Smith shares her wisdom, knowledge, and experience in a way that gives us greater understanding to our own personal journey as well as the strength and courage to face the many challenges and expectations that come with the professional mixture of marriage and ministry.

As the wife of a man who is a preacher and a professor, and as a woman involved in writing, teaching, and leading large groups of pastor's wives for the past twenty-five years (in Beeson Divinity School's sponsored annual Pastor's School), I am well acquainted with the challenges that can come from that confusing role. Dr. Taylor-Smith discusses the problems the pastor's wife can face and gives answers that instruct, explain, and encourage us as women today.

Authors most often have particular reasons that drive them to purposely commit the necessary and intensive time, thought, and energy into writing a book. Wanda Taylor-Smith wrote this book because she discovered a lack of literature devoted to the unique roles of the preacher's wife, especially the African American preacher's wife. She saw the "felt need" for this volume as she watched a community of Christian women struggle with their own identities, personhoods, and vocations in the workplace and alongside a pastor-husband in the church.

Using the New Testament example of Priscilla, Wanda Taylor-Smith shows the competent woman as a Christian believer; a true and equal partner to her husband, Aquila, in ministry and in business (tent making); a professor teaching the Gospel proclamation; and an intelligent, strong, and responsible woman for whom the Apostle Paul had great respect and admiration.

The author interviewed twenty African American women whose husbands were Protestant pastors. They spoke honestly and openly. The author's recorded findings are both fascinating and enlightening. About their roles as pastor's wives, the women used words like "wonderful," "challenging," "rough," "rewarding," "good," and "bad." Many mentioned the stress and hurt the role caused them. Others confessed differing feelings of happiness and sadness, pain and sorrow, and pleasure and joy. The women speak of the unavoidable stress (*distress*) that can result from home, church, and community relationships and ministry and the challenging perseverance required to fulfill perfectly the roles of wife, mother, grandmother, community leader, and, in many cases, the church's "First Lady." Added to all of that is the pressure to somehow fulfill these roles and be the *textbook example* to other women, mothers, wives, etc.

I believe one of the most enlightening and helpful chapters in this book (Chapter Six) is the explanation of role adaptability in which she provides eye-opening descriptions of the six different ways women can respond to their unique circumstances. She explains each type of response classification (embracers, enlightened compromisers, resigned compromisers, defiant compromisers, independents, and defiant resisters) and shows how each applies to the pastor's wife. Brilliant.

I recommend that every pastor's wife as well as every person in the congregation — including her pastor-husband and the church staff — read this book. It will help the pastor's wife better understand herself, her challenges, and her roles. And it will show the congregation, the church staff, and her husband the difficult position she has willingly accepted — that is the recognition of her own call to vocational ministry and the challenges such a position presents to **her.** With greater understanding about the role of the pastor's wife, my hope is that she can find greater support and practical help as she fulfills her own call to ministry and life.

Denise George
Author of *What Women Wish Pastors Knew* (Zondervan) and
What Pastors Wish Church Members Knew (Zondervan);
international speaker;
married to Dr. Timothy George, founding dean
of Beeson Divinity School,
Samford University, professor and former pastor

Acknowledgements

Without the twenty women married to pastors whose stories serve as the basis, this book would not be. I pray that the presentation of each of your stories is as you intended and that your willingness to share your wisdom will bless many others.

Thank you to all of the women who endorsed the book and to the men who contributed to the epilogue section. Your words of encouragement to me and to others are greatly appreciated.

I must also thank my daughter and granddaughters Lawren Nunn and the Nunn sisters, Kayla, Jordan and Rhyan, who provided much comic relief and pleasant distraction during the tense time of the production of this book.

There are many who have provided encouragement and support along the way to bring this book into existence. I wish to express my gratitude to each one but space will not permit. However, you know who you are.

But the one who has pushed and prodded, pulled and prompted me the most to make the book happen is my partner in marriage and ministry, Dr. Robert Smith, Jr. Thank you for your love for me and for your faith in me to see "the not yet" as if it were "the already."

To Him who sits on the throne and to the Lamb be praise and honor
and glory and power forever and ever.
Revelation 5:13 (NIV)

Introduction

Most women have a story that begs to be told. This book is an attempt to tell the story of a particular group of women: women who are married to preachers, or pastors. (For the purpose of this book, the single term "pastor" is used for uniformity, but the message contained therein can also be useful for women who are married to men who are preachers, clergymen, ministry leaders or missionaries.) Almost every woman in this group has struggled with issues that are related to her role as "the preacher's wife" or "ministry wife." Some women have been able to flourish in the role; others have succumbed to the pressures encountered in the role and have been crushed under the weight. Yet others have given up and left not only the ministry but also the marriage.

Women who have not experienced any such painful struggles may find this book useful to help understand the hurt of some of their fellow sisters in Christ. It will sensitize one to those who have been wounded by people and events encountered in their journeys as women married to men who have been called to preach God's word and even to shepherd His people.

The recording of the accounts of these women accomplishes several things. First, it brings awareness to the women as individual persons who are separate from their husbands. Second, it breaks down the walls of isolation, which many women build, by letting them know they are not alone in their struggle. Third, it serves as a reference to increase understanding and support from husbands and others who need enlightenment in this area.

This is not a book of "how to" or "ten steps to wholeness." It is a book that "breaks the silence" and gives a voice to women who have long borne their burden in quiet isolation, and often desperation, in an attempt to serve their Lord and His people.

This is not written as a Bible study; however, there are biblical references and examples. Although it is not a Bible study, it can be used as a basis for group discussions. My hope and prayer is that it will help somebody—that women will read it and say, "Yes! That is how I feel; I didn't know anyone else felt that way!" From there she can move, with God's help, to confidence in whom God has created her to be. Or perhaps it may prompt someone else to say, "Now I have a better understanding of how she feels," which will enable that husband/friend/family member/congregant to be a better support for the woman as she follows God's path for her life.

The narrative begins with the account of the awakening of my awareness to the plight of many of the women who are married to pastors along with a bit of my own story. Biblical character Priscilla is then presented as a paradigm or model for learning. The diagnosis or examination of the role as perceived by the women in the study is discussed followed by a prescription for the diagnosis or findings given though the voices of the women using the paradigm or teaching model derived from Priscilla's example. The women in the study group then give important pointers for women coming into the role. To aid in the assessment of the degree of adaptation to the role, a typology, or way of categorizing, is presented. Because there is often confusion about the value of women in God's sight, a chapter on the topic is included. At the end the voice from the perspective of the other partner in the ministry dyad—the husband—is heard through commentaries from several seasoned men who have been called to preach God's word.

CHAPTER ONE

Breaking the Silence

In February 1996 I was a speaker at the National Conference for Ministry Wives in Orlando, Florida. During one of the sessions, "How to Feel Up in a Down World" by Barbara Holmes, the wives were asked to form teams of two to share and pray with each other about any pressing life issues. I was paired with a woman from Michigan who was married to a pastor. After talking and praying for each other, I leaned over the bench and gave her a hug. She burst into tears as she held on tightly. When I asked her what had prompted this emotional response, she stated, "That was the first hug I have had from anyone outside of my family in years. Thank you!" I was stunned!

This encounter with a fellow ministry wife prompted me to begin to look at this group of women from a different perspective: the perspective of the woman as an individual. This perspective focused on the untold experience of the woman rather than on her marital relationship or on how she functions. The center of attention was to be the woman as a person. What had caused such isolation? Why the seemingly huge volume of pent-up emotion that could be released by a mere hug? The emotional response from the woman seemed to be an indication of loneliness and isolation from others. How could this lack be identified and rectified? The desire was born in me to take a closer look to determine how a woman could come to this point.

People have always been curious about the lives of other people. Long, in her book *Telling Women's Lives* relates how she became deeply engrossed in the telling of women's lives. Her curiosity led to efforts to "identify the elements of a woman-centered methodology for telling women's lives…" (1999, 117). I, likewise, because of the revelation in Florida and fueled by my own experiences, became interested in the "telling of women's lives," specifically women who are married to pastors. I became more intentional in my interactions with these women in various settings. Because I often traveled with my preacher/professor husband, there had been ample opportunities to dialogue with many of these women of varied backgrounds, cultures, ages, locations, and situations. In the conversations questions began to emerge. How do the women in the role deal with the expectations of this role? Does the woman who is married to a preacher, pastor, clergyman, ministry leader, or missionary view her role as different from the role of any other woman married to a man with a profession? What are some of the blessings? What are some of the challenges? How are these handled effectively? What wisdom would each want to pass on to others who are facing similar situations?

My story, as is everyone's story, is unique to me. But many may find enough similarities to their stories to identify with the experience. I had planned to become a nurse since I was in junior high school. Before wanting to become a nurse, I had thought of being a veterinarian. Those thoughts were dashed when I discovered I would be required to care for snakes and birds, not just cats and dogs.

Though I had planned to become a nurse and realized that career goal, I had not planned to become a pastor's wife. My sentiments on the matter were the same as Wilma Bachus notes in her book *Called to the Ministry of Pastor's Wife*: "I never wanted to be a preacher's wife, and I certainly had no desire to become a pastor's wife. I wanted to be a Christian and live a good Christian life." (2005, 11).

But because of my strong faith in God, I followed His leading into that very role when I married the widowed pastor of a medium-sized congregation. Not only did I instantly become "the pastor's wife," I also became the stepmother to three sons. We were then a blended family of six, including my daughter from a previous marriage.

My nursing background in direct patient and family care and in management has been a valuable resource for functioning in the complex dynamics inherent in the roles of parent, stepparent, and pastor's and professor's wife. In my nursing career, I have had to interact with people, both male and female of all ages, in myriad circumstances that ranged from birth to death while dealing with the range of human response to these multitudinous circumstances from joy to suicidal or homicidal threats or actual attempts. For example there were many times during our children's teenage years when I had to draw upon my knowledge of adolescent behaviors. There were times when recalling group facilitation skills learned during management seminars was of great service when conducting ministry and committee meetings. Members of the congregation often assumed that, because I was a nurse, I had full and complete knowledge of every medication and ailment known to them and, therefore, they often sought advice on any related matter. Learning how to respond professionally to different people in so many different situations in striving for positive outcomes prepared me for the demands of being a parent and the wife of a dedicated and sincere pastor and professor.

Being a woman married to a preacher for over twenty-five years has provided an opportunity to experience simultaneously the dual role of having a personal profession while being the wife of the pastor. Thus the experience has heightened my interest in the various responses of my "sisters." I have been intrigued by the wide range of interpretations, expectations, and manifestations of the role itself and how the women perceive themselves in the role of "the preacher's wife." In attempting to find investigative literature on the topic of the role of the preacher's wife, I soon discovered a lack, particularly on the African American woman's experience. Thus I felt led to address the void by researching this particular experience.

From discussions with women married to pastors from different ethnic origins from across the country, several themes emerged concerning the role of women married to pastors. The consensus was that the role is stressful. The perception of the women in previous discussions was that there is an added dimension to the role-induced stress which is based on two circumstances. First, there exists uniqueness to this particular spousal role, and second, the relationship of the role with one's faith is very significant.

One of the greatest travesties or injustices to women who are married to pastors and to women in general is to tell them who they *supposedly* are and not who they *really* are. It is *not* who people say you are but rather it *is* who God has created you to be. In the beginning the original status of the female was equal in importance to the male. But since the Fall, there seems to be some confusion as to the relevance of women.

Women are not men. Although that may seem, at first glance, to be an obvious statement, women have been lost in the word "men" for some time. Women are not "less than," but they are "different." That is not a negative; that is the way God created us — to be different. The Bible says that God created male and female (Genesis 1:27). He created Eve, female, as a suitable mate for Adam, male. She was made to be a mate for, and not an imitation or copy of, Adam. A mate in this sense is intended to be a completion of a pair. In most cases women are not trying to be men; women just want the same respect as an equal creation of God and to have a personal choice to exercise their abilities rather than have restrictions that are not reasonable.

Now we will look at a woman who perhaps shares some similar concerns. Priscilla of the Bible was a first-century woman with a twenty-first-century lifestyle. How can an examination of her life speak to the woman of today? What made her effective then? Can those same approaches be useful now?

Chapter Two

$\mathcal{HER}$-meneutics: Priscilla, a Phenomenal Woman

The meaning of the word *hermeneutics* is merely "the interpretation of a text." In this case we are interpreting the text of the life of a person—Priscilla. We find Priscilla primarily in Acts 18, but she is also mentioned in Romans 16:3, 1 Corinthians 16:19, and 2 Timothy 4:19. Priscilla, or Prisca, a Roman name, is reported to mean "worthy or venerable" or "ancient, old-fashioned simplicity." Born in Pontus, Italy, approximately two thousand years ago, she was a woman who exhibited in the first century some of the same roles in which women find themselves in the twenty-first century. James A. Sanders, a professor of canonical hermeneutics, said, "Most biblical texts must be read, not by looking in them for models for morality, but by looking in them for mirrors for identity" (1976, 157). Priscilla provides a mirror for identity for women married to pastors.

Priscilla and her husband, Aquila, were expelled from Rome by Emperor Claudius Caesar along with all other Jewish people at that time. They settled in Corinth where they connected with Apostle Paul who writes of their story in Acts 18. The facts that they connected, that Paul stayed in their home and later they followed him to Ephesus, indicate that although they were Jews, they had prior knowledge of The Way of Christ and the doctrine of grace. Priscilla and Aquila are routinely mentioned together; sometimes Priscilla is listed first, and other times Aquila's name appears first. The "P and A Ministry, Inc." is an enlightening reflection for modern day ministry couples, particularly the women, due to six revealed characteristics.

First, Priscilla was a **person**—she was mentioned by her name. Although she is primarily mentioned along with her husband, she is not buried in his identity; she stands as her own person with God-given skills and knowledge that she uses to advance His kingdom. She neither appears demeaned or slighted below her worth because she is a woman nor is she exalted for the same reason. She is who she is, who God created her to be.

Second, Priscilla was a "**professer**" as well as a **professor**—she had professed her belief in this new religion—Christianity. She had knowledge of the Jewish heritage law as well as the coming of Christ resulting in the law transformed by grace. She believed in and supported the gospel demonstrated by the opening of her home to Paul as he served in the Corinth area. According to 1 Corinthians 16:19, there was also a church that met in their home. It was apparent that she had a personal relationship with her Lord and that her faith was strong and based in correct theology.

Priscilla became a **professor** when she, along with her husband, invited Apollos to their home to instruct him privately on the new dispensation of Christ. The fact that it was done privately should not be overlooked. This demonstrated wise sensitivity to the person, Apollos, and to the proclamation that there would be no public argument among believers that would detract from the word and work of God. Priscilla was willing to share her knowledge with another to help that person advance as a Christian.

Third, Priscilla was a **partner** — there is true partnership in ministry between the couple Aquila and Priscilla. Equality as well as equity is demonstrated in marriage and in ministry. Priscilla was included equally in the narrative and was given importance, equity, when included. When the expulsion occurred, they went together to Corinth. There is no mention of children, yet there is no indication that Priscilla was depreciated in value as a person because she had no children. When Paul went to Ephesus, both Aquila and Priscilla went with him. She was not left behind in Corinth to take care of the household or keep the business going at that location. In Ephesus, when Apollos was noted to have incomplete knowledge of "the way of God," they instructed him together in the home they shared. As mentioned previously their names routinely are linked together when listed in the Bible (Acts 18:2, 18, and 26; Romans 16:3; 1 Corinthians 16:19 and 2 Timothy 4:19).

Priscilla's shared equity with her husband did not seem to give Paul the same difficulty or pause as indicated by his later admonishments to women. He accepted her both as Aquila's marital partner and as his ministry partner. He spoke of Priscilla with great respect in each of his greetings to her and her husband after he had left their vicinity. There was no mention of the need for her to limit her presence in the partnership with her husband — no relegation of her to the shadow of her husband in the marriage or in the ministry.

Fourth, Priscilla was a **producer** — she worked alongside her husband in their trade which was tent making (Acts 18:3). She was a working woman; she had a trade that contributed to the financial well-being of the household. She was not a wilting violet who stayed in the home, the "private sphere," with no interaction with the "public sphere."

She and her husband must have been financially stable. They had a home while living in Rome. When expelled, they were able to travel to Corinth from Rome and to obtain their own home there when they arrived. Later they were able to book passage to Ephesus and obtain another home in Ephesus. Those activities—travel and homeownership—required substantial funds then just as they do today and possibly even more so. There were no credit cards—you had to have tangible means to pay in that day.

Again, it should be noted that Paul had nothing but respect for her as a woman who worked, for he worked *with* her and her husband. Paul did not recommend that she was out of line because she worked and contributed to the economy of the household. He did not restrict her to the kitchen or to servitude to her husband.

Fifth, Priscilla was **pliant**—not that she was easily influenced or bent but that she was adaptable and receptive to change. Priscilla moved from Pontus, Italy, where she was reportedly born, to Rome, also in Italy, to Corinth, the area that is now Greece. From Greece she moved with her husband to Ephesus in Asia Minor, the area that is now in the country of Turkey. Paul later sends a greeting to her and Aquila indicating that she had returned to Rome (Romans 16:3). She was able to adapt to and flourish in each locale in which she and her husband settled. It is not recorded that she complained about the packing up and moving and unpacking and setting up a home so many times. She appeared able to flourish in all three countries and cultures. She seemed to recognize that what was happening to her and Aquila was much bigger than both of them and that it was important for the work and spread of this new gospel. It was a true "going with the flow" for the kingdom of God. It seemed that the excitement of being a part of such a great movement overcame the inconvenience of such frequent uprooting.

Sixth, Priscilla demonstrated **perseverance**—she was open to the travel across three countries on two continents. In that day travel was nothing like the travel of today. People did not routinely travel for pleasure but mainly out of necessity, such as for business. Unlike today travel was not done in the luxury of a comfortable mode of transportation. Whether over land or water, it was a rather arduous and sometimes dangerous journey (Gower 1987). Can you imagine what it must have been like to travel in those days? Picture no clean rest stops along the road and no "facilities" on the boats. On land you had to walk or ride in a cart with no springs or on a horse, donkey, mule, or camel, and there was no air conditioning or protection from the sun, wind, or rain. Since roads were not normally paved, the way was less than smooth, and the number of animals traveling along the route made it less than fragrant. On the sea your accommodations would have been in tight quarters shared most often with the cargo. Since the boats were small in comparison to the ships we know today and had no stabilizers to steady the boat, the effects of the waves on the sea were much more evident. On land or on the sea, passengers had to bring their own provisions. It took a strong woman to endure such travel several times.

Person, "professer" and professor, partner, producer, one who was pliant and who persevered; how can these characteristics speak to women today who are married to pastors? What needs expressed by the women can be met by the cultivation of some of these attributes?

CHAPTER THREE

Diagnosis

As a registered nurse who worked in the field of women's health for thirty-four years, I have seen the complexities of finding a diagnosis for a condition. A clinical diagnosis is "made from a study of the signs and symptoms of a condition" (Randolph 1994). In an attempt to examine the experience of women who are married to pastors, I had to seek the signs and symptoms—the issues that seem to be inherent to these women. Using research literature on women in general and on women specific to this group, along with conversations of women in the role, certain "signs and symptoms" emerged.

What is presented in this book is what I learned from those sources and expressed through the words of interviews with twenty women from a wide range in ages, role experiences, and locations. Although these women were African American women whose husbands were

Protestant pastors, their stories and experiences can serve to enlighten both women and men across cultures, denominations, and settings. Their stories apply to women who are married to pastors and those women who hope to do so.

The Personal Perception of the Role

When asked to describe their experiences of being women who are married to pastors, the women usually gave pensive and thoughtful responses. There were always positives that outweighed the negatives. Regardless of the number of challenges encountered, most of the women were honored that God chose them for this particular ministry. Several of the women referred to the ministry of being married to a pastor as a "calling." **Naomi** responded:

> I've been told by pastors' wives that the Lord called *him*—not them—so as long as they're present that's all that's needed of them....(They say,) 'Don't ask me to be involved—I'm there—that's all that's needed.' I totally disagree with that. And I just believe if God called him, He called you because the two of you are one. That it's one unit...it comes with the call.

Claudia agreed. "When he said in his initial sermon that God had called him, I knew God called me, too—not to preach but to be his wife. So I have to tell women that. It's a calling on you, too."

Granted, some have come to that conclusion only after years of growing in their faith. At first some expressed inadequacy: "...then when he accepted the call...I was always wondering would I be able to handle it....that was a big calling. Am I worthy of this grand distinction?"(**Damaris**). Others initially expressed doubt: "I was one of those ladies that said, 'God called him but not me.' But now I'm at a point that I know that God, if He called him and I was his wife, then He called me to serve *with* him" (**Esther**).

I have had many conversations with women concerning their experiences of being married to pastors. Several common themes seem to arise from their conversations that deal with their own personal descriptions of the role.

Many of the women used words that are on complete opposite ends of the spectrum of feeling and being to describe the experience of being married to a pastor. They spoke of their own personal experiences in terms that would seem oxymoronic in nature, using words that do not appear to go together. **Esther** stated:

It is a lot of things mixed up in one. It's a pleasure sometimes and a joy…sometimes it's a burden and sometimes it's stressful. It's a combination of things that tends to even itself out in the long run—being stressful and hurtful, and then there's joy and happiness.

Eunice used two additional opposite terms: "It's bittersweet. You have great benefits…but you have to sacrifice." Though there are times of highs and lows, **Huldah** considered the good outweighs the bad: "I would say it's days of extreme joy and many challenges…I have had more joy than challenges." Several other women expressed the same sentiments using seemingly opposing terms. **Jochebed, Miriam, Phoebe,** and **Priscilla** used such phrases as "wonderful at times, challenging at times"; "it was rough and rewarding"; "good and bad"; and "happiness and sadness, pain and sorrow, pleasure and joy."

Expectations

Expectations—we all have them. An expectation is something that is looked forward to, something that is supposed or thought of as being a future event or occurrence or condition, to consider due or necessary. We are all confronted with multiple expectations in the various realms or compartments of our lives. Those expectations can be associated with any one, or possibly more than one, of the myriad roles in which we as women see ourselves or are seen by others. We are daughters, aunts, mothers, grandmothers, friends, cousins, nieces, neighbors, co-workers, supervisors, committee chairs, committee members, etc.

There are certain expectations associated with being married to a pastor. **The women believe that there are many expectations that are placed upon them merely because of the one to whom they are married.** According to Joyce Landorf Heatherly in her book *Balcony People*, "She *must* be spiritual at all times, with a handy biblical reference on the tip of her tongue. She must never have a bad day and lose her spirit or her temper, and most of all, she *must* be able to play the piano" (1994, 65). The topic of expectations by far drew the greatest response and list of manifestations. This topic can be broken down into categories and then into subcategories.

External and Internal

In the classic book *Great Expectations* by Charles Dickens (1861/1985), the main character, Pip, is buffeted and beleaguered by several unfortunate events that affect the course of his life. Those events carried with them myriad events that were forecasted for his life; some positive, some negative. These great expectations faced by Pip were divided into two major categories: external and internal. As with Pip, we face expectations or assumptions which originate externally from others along with those which arise internally from within our own selves.

The *external messages* can come from husbands, children, friends, co-workers, congregation members, family members, and others. But we also have ideas in our own heads about who we are and what we should do: *internal messages*. Where do these ideas come from? Many come from our upbringing, something we have read, or possibly other women we have known who are married to pastors. Whether the expectation was external or internal, there were themes or subcategories into which they could be grouped according to the nature of the expectation.

Attire and Appearance

The most common theme in this area was **the supposed attire of the woman married to a pastor.** It was expected that she be well-groomed and appropriately dressed at all times. For the woman married to a pastor in the African American church (the "First Lady," a title frequently assigned to her), the controversy primarily surrounded the tradition for the woman to wear "the hat" and to dress impeccably. **Naomi** said, "I think that people expect the pastor's wife...to be this person who...sits on the front row with a big hat." **Jochebed** agreed that many of the congregants held that opinion: "There were a lot of members who thought this...I should dress or wear my hats." **Damaris** did not yield to the pressure of the expectation: "They expect you to wear that hat that I absolutely refuse to."

Even if the question of the traditional hat was not raised, there seemed to be a certain level of elegance in attire that needed to be met for those married to pastors. **Eunice** referred to the expectation as having "to dress to the nines all the time." **Miriam** said, "They expect you to wear certain things." But **Dorcas** indicated that there are also certain criteria for the certain things: "I think they felt that you had to dress really nice and be in the latest fashion, not wear the same dress twice and all of that."

Excellent Example

Along with looking the part, the women expressed displeasure in the expectation of having certain behaviors. It was as if they were given a certain part to play. The part was that of being an *excellent example* by the consistent display of leadership, presence at all requested functions, godly behavior, and the ability to instruct others on all biblical matters. Having biblical knowledge, not an unreasonable expectation, was not so much the problem, but what they did find objectionable was the level of expertise required of them. It was thought to be above that which was required of others merely because she was married to a pastor. "They expect you to know the Word, and naturally you should if you're a Christian...you should know something about the Word," commented **Lydia**.

For women whose husbands are senior pastors, there are addition-al **desired behaviors and abilities. Damaris** stated, "They want (you) to be a leader...to be knowledgeable...to be comforting, encouraging, and supportive." **Eunice** echoed her sentiments concerning the desires of the congregants — that she should represent them (the congregants) in perfection: "You don't need to be sitting in the back. You represent (your church), you need to sit up front." The concept of representing the congregation is repeated by **Lois**: "That I represent them well...to be honest and real...to be a teacher and leader, an example and some-one who can hold a confidence...to pray for them...to study the Word... to train, to nurture, to love..." According to **Esther**:

> The church expects me...to attend all the services and be involved in all activities of the church...I should be able to be there for them, to talk to them. I should be able to lead them if they have a question in some discussion...they expect me to know the Bible back and front...

Esther also noted that it is not just the members of the congregation who have expectations: "The people in the community expect me...to be helpful, to act in a Christian way." **Jehosheba** expands the source of expectations even further: "I think society as a whole puts expectations on you. Whether they are churched or unchurched people, it's a whole different standard that they hold you up to when they know you are pastor's wife."

Not only was the expectation for perfection placed upon the par-ticipants and their husbands, but there were also expectations imposed upon the children. This proscriptive (restrictive) attitude which placed pressure on the children caused the women more concern than the expectations that were placed upon the women personally. According to **Abigail,** "…they're looking at not just me and my husband, they're looking at the children as well… and it's as if we are above reproach… that we can't do anything wrong." **Miriam** agreed, "They expect your children to be perfect." **Claudia** declared, "I had to let them know they're children just like yours. Don't expect anything out of them that you wouldn't expect out of yours. Let the children be children." **Persis's** heated reply to the question "Your kids go to parties?" was "Yes. They're kids, so they go to kids' parties with other fifteen and sixteen year olds. And *you're* not going to make them have to stay at home because they're the preacher's kids…you are not going to do that to them!"

Satisfactory Substitute

Several women noted another presumptive expectation that is manifested with regard to the women who are married to pastors. That expectation is **the assumed ability to serve as a capable and acceptable substitute in the absence or unavailability of the husband.** This phenomenon is unknown in any other study of expectation of wives. To ask women married to lawyers, doctors, athletes, or construction workers to stand in when the husband is not available would be unthinkable. The closest situation to that of women married to pastors is probably that of women married to diplomats or to politicians who are asked to step in on primarily social events. **Claudia** remarked that in the case of hospital visits, "Sometimes they will say, 'I know Pastor's not here, but…would you go with me?'" **Miriam** related the same when it was a request for prayer: "In certain situations, people expect *me*…if my husband is not available, they'll say that they want me, then I'll go." For issues that arise around the church, **Damaris** declared that she is the designated substitute: "If they need the pastor to give them something and he's not around, then they'll look to me."

Assumed Talents and Gifts

Often the congregation and community at large also **attribute certain talents and gifts to women who are married to pastors that they do not necessarily possess.** Some of the women even expressed regret that they did not have these talents that would enable them to meet the expectations. There was the expectation of being musically gifted either in voice or instrument. "They expect you to be able to be a musician—but I'm not..." (**Lydia**). "My other friends (pastors' wives) play the organ. They play music and they sing. So I thought maybe I should be doing something" (**Jochebed**). **Eunice** agreed: "They expect you to be able to sing..." **Jehosheba** also concurred: "Everybody thinks you should be a singer, playing the piano...teaching—church members think that you should do anything that they don't want to do."

Another expected talent along with being musically gifted was that the woman be an eloquent and prepared speaker. "Some of the expectations are that I always have something to say—that I have an impromptu speech that's perfect for the occasion and the moment," claimed **Lois.**

While some of the participants report an expectation of presence at events and active involvement in church ministry, other participants felt **an expectation of silence and of a spectator stance. Lydia** made this observation: "As far as speaking and having voting privileges and things like that, sometimes I find that they want you to just be quiet." **Persis** indicated that the silence that was preferable, particularly for the senior pastor's wife, was passed down from a prior era. "The older generation had the idea that the pastor's wife should be quiet and unassuming and just smile a lot and not have a voice." **Phoebe** added that the "...pastors' wives (are looked upon) as the person that is in the background...."

Husband/Family/Job

The expectations that originated from the husbands had to do with being loving companions, supporting their ministries, and caring for the home and family. The requirements from these areas, though not as uncomfortable or strenuous, would at times cause some level of stress. **Dorcas** gave a comprehensive statement of expectations from her husband:

> I think my husband expects me to rubber stamp everything that he says in public....I think mostly the expectations he has of me also come from being not so much a pastor's wife, but being a Christian woman, loving the Lord, and those things that I would do as a Christian woman who loves the Lord and is walking in faith....I think his expectations of me are to honor him and respect him and not do anything to shame the name of Christ or to shame him.

Others spoke of the desire of the husband for them to be active in a joint ministry and to care for the family. **Lydia** stated:

> He expects me to be…supportive of him, to be by his side, and, of course, to be knowledgeable of the Word…to be a part of his ministry, to let people know that we are one. To be a mother, to be a good wife…to have a vital role in the community, in our home, and in the church…

Naomi claimed that her husband "…expects that I'm there on Sundays…that I'm in tune with what he's saying…and with what is going on in the service so that if he calls me up and needs assistance for prayer, I'm right there." **Priscilla's** husband informed her that he was "looking for someone who will support him throughout his ministry." With laughter, **Miriam** stated about her husband, "He expects dinner!"

The family members and coworkers also weighed in on the "should do" list with expectations of behaviors for the women based on the fact that their husbands are pastors. **Esther** shared the tradition in her family of one particular duty of the wife: "There were expectations from my family of what a wife should be…when I would go visit my aunt…she would say, 'Get up and fix him (the husband) a plate.'" Even people in the work setting had some preconceived ideas that assigned certain duties on the role title alone. **Julia** said, "I went to a retirement luncheon (on the job). Because I'm married to a minister, without warning they said, 'We're going to have Mrs. ___ do the invocation and grace.'"

Self

The self expectations, whether realistic or unrealistic, originated from the women's own ideas of who they should be or how they should act. Sometimes the idealized self was based in her biblical understanding of a "Christian woman." **Lois** related:

What I expect myself to do is the right and godly thing, to grow, to be strong enough and committed enough to push aside anything self-centered or anything that's not God-like in the way I do things…that I never lose sight of what is expected of me by God. Because of His Word that tells me 'I can do all things through Christ who strengthens me'… My expectation is to grow more and more in this ministry; to be a greater witness for Him and to truly be an evangelist.

Other times it was grounded in her perception of who she should be and what she should do based on observations of other, oftentimes more senior women who were married to pastors. **Jochebed** admits that she fell into this category. "I had some problems with myself… because I have a lot of pastors' wives that do these things…Well, what I was doing was comparing myself."

Aloneness vs. Loneliness/Isolation

Heatherley, in her book *Balcony People,* relates what she noted when speaking at a luncheon for women married to pastors: "I saw their immense loneliness; I felt the chill of their discouragement; and I knew the aroma of rejection which clung to their skin like a pungent perfume" (1994, 64). One of the "side effects" of being a woman married to a pastor is frequently the presence of a feeling of being alone, of being lonely, or of being isolated. Although all three conditions may appear to be the same, there is a difference, and one can experience them singularly or in any combination.

Being alone is defined as "apart from others, being separated from." This is not always a bad thing; one may want to be alone at times but usually not *all* of the time and then at one's own discretion. "Lonely" implies that the condition of being alone or separate from others — whether physically, mentally, or emotionally — produces a feeling of sadness and increases stress. One can be lonely in a crowd of people when there is no feeling of connection or community with others. Isolation is a huge step beyond being alone and can certainly produce loneliness. When one is isolated, there is not only separation but there is some form of barrier to maintain the separation, whether it is actual or imagined.

The woman at the Florida conference who had not had a hug from anyone outside of her family in a long time was feeling lonely *and* isolated. She did not say that there was no one around her; it was that there was little or no connection to any of those persons outside of her family. **Naomi** stated that, when at church she often sees that "there is nobody on my row…I don't know if they feel that we are untouchable or what." When speaking of the woman married to a pastor, **Abigail** said, "I see her as someone who can be very lonely because she can't share everything with everyone. There are very few people that she can confide in, any personal thoughts or situations…Sometimes it is a lonely role." "There is so much hurt and pain and you can't talk to anybody about it. That's the thing — who do you talk to?" queried **Lois**.

Some of the women note that they are often alone when their husbands are pulled away to deal with ministry needs. This was particularly difficult when there were children in the home. If the husband was a senior pastor or ministry leader, it was a more frequent occurrence, as he had the responsibility of overseeing the congregation or that particular ministry. **Damaris** noted:

> There are times when I wish he had more flexible time to be with family and to do different personal things like when we have family reunion. Sometimes I have to go without him, and those are sometimes difficult times, but I understand he has a duty. Over the years you learn to adjust. We learn to adapt to whatever the schedule.

Loss of Self or Personhood

Papanek, in her study of men, women, and work, reported that women are often subsumed into, lost in, or swallowed up in the occupations of their husbands in what she calls a "two-person single career." She described the "two-person career" as a middle-class pattern in which the "wife is neither formally employed nor remunerated (paid) in any direct sense" (1973, 857). In this phenomenon, she observed, the institution which employs only the husband also places both formal and informal demands on the wife — "two-for-one." However, the economics of the present time have made it difficult for a single-wage earner to support the average "middle-class" family. According to the Bureau of Labor Statistics, in 2011 women accounted for 47 percent of all employed persons sixteen years of age and older (up from 33.9 percent in 1950 but down from 59 percent in 2007). This same source says that the median percent contribution of the women to the family income has risen from 26.6 percent to 37.1 percent from 1970 to 2009.

The income from the woman has become a larger portion of the overall income for the family.

Taylor and Hartley (1975) applied this same concept of "two-for-one" to the Protestant ministry. However, there is a major divergence. As with other women, the economic climate for women married to pastors has also changed. Of the women interviewed for my study, 80 percent were currently working or were retired from working outside of the home. Contrary to the report of Papanek in 1973, many women of today are gainfully employed in paid positions and careers rather than being "gainfully *un*employed" as she suggested.

Therefore, the woman may have a career outside of the home as well as maintaining the home, possibly parenting children, and being a mate for the husband while being supportive to his ministry in varying degrees. **Jochebed** remembers tough times: "I was the only one working. I was working eight hours, coming home to do another eight hour job—cooking and taking care of the children...So that was very stressful for me...I trust God, but still I'm human." **Miriam** says, "... sometimes I look back, and I wonder how I did it all...managing the time and the dates and everything at home...it was hard. But it was manageable." All of this and the woman is then routinely indistinctly referred to as "the wife of...," "the Pastor's wife," or "...and his wife." Being a wife is a highly honorable role ordained by God and much desired by many women; however, "the wife" has a name just as the husband has a name. Just as with the husband, her name sets her apart as an individual. Often the woman who is married seems to lose her name and her associated identity as an individual when she is referred to as a "tag-on" to her husband, particularly when the husband is serving as a pastor.

Along those same lines, often there were characteristics bestowed upon the women that further demonstrate this failure to see the women as individuals. Interestingly, each bestowed image or imagined characteristic was presented as a negative even though the characteristic alone would be considered a positive one. An example is that the woman may be thought to be "holy," "quiet and modest," and a "biblical scholar." Though these are admirable qualities in any Christian, the women took exception to the blanket application of these traits to *all* women married to pastors. **Claudia** stated, "Sometimes I think they view her as different…not being a person that you can have fun with or not even a person that you can be friends with…they view her as a *role* instead of a *person*." **Hannah** responded with an insight to the cause of such stereotypes of women married to pastors: "They don't take time to get to know the wife…they don't see her as a person that they can talk to. They don't think that that person is down to earth, they think that she is upon a pedestal." **Huldah** concurred with Hannah when she said, "They don't see them as individuals, they (paint the picture with) a broad brush…that all pastors' wives sing or play the piano or wear a big hat. A misconception—they don't take the individual case by case…"

Other Concerns Specific to Women Married to Pastors

Other assumptions mentioned involved financial security, marital bliss, model children, and an elitist attitude with the appearance of a perfect life. **Hannah** stated that people assume "that the church is giving us a lot of money…" **Lois** said, "They assume that we have it easy… They figure that (the pastor) has two jobs and we get all our finances taken care of." Contrary to the assumption of having financial stability and marital calm, **Miriam** indicated that is not always the case: "They assume that you have money when you don't…they assume that your marriage is perfect…that you don't have the common problems that other people have…"

It was perceived by others that the women lived ideal lives—lives that embodied all that any woman would desire in a marriage and home devoid of difficulties of any kind. **Naomi** expressed exasperation when she related what others have indicated:

> …that my life is just A-OK—perfect all the time…that I don't have problems…they assume that because I'm married to the pastor that all is okay; I'm just right there with God, and I just got the perfect life, and everything is wonderful…that I don't cry…me and the pastor don't have issues like any other couple.

Succinctly put, some congregants think, "She's lucky—she's married to Pastor; what kind of problems could *she* have?" (**Persis**). Because people view the role from the outside, **Abigail** concluded that they are not aware of the sameness in some of life's difficulties when she stated:

> They assume that it's an easy role. That we…don't have a care and a cross and our children are always obedient—they never make a mistake…they just have no idea that we face the same problems, disappointments, and tribulations that they face.

Stress

The combination of the expressed concerns, myriad expectations, loneliness/isolation, loss of self, and other bestowed characteristics and assumptions tend to increase the stress experienced by the women. **Esther** says of being married to a pastor, "…sometimes it's stressful, very stressful."

Stress is universal in occurrence but not uniform in experience or response. Although all humans, and many other living organisms, display a stress response in some fashion, these responses are not demonstrated in the same way or to the same degree. Neither do all humans characterize the same stimuli as a stressor or threat. The terms "women" and "stress" are two words that are often found in conjunction with one another. It is as if, to paraphrase a once popular song, you can't have one (women) without the other (stress).

As early as the fourteenth century, the term "stress" was found with a meaning of "hardship, or adversity, affliction". Selye used the term "stress" to denote a force exerted on an individual that "might alter an individual's ability to respond or react differently" (Selye, 1956). Stress in itself cannot be categorized as only good or only bad. The description of stress as good or bad is largely situational and circumstantial. According to Selye the good stress, known as "eustress," is the response that helps the individual deal with the stimulus, threat, or stressor effectively. It is the reaction that fuels the energy and performance ability to accomplish daunting tasks. This is the stress that pushes one to finish pending duties and finish them well. However, when the level of stress passes the point of enhancing function, it then becomes dysfunctional and is known as "distress." Distress or dysfunctional stress can influence the physical, emotional, and spiritual facets of the human experience, surfacing as hypertension, ulcers, insomnia, fatigue, headaches, apathy, irritability, and anxiety disorders (Selye, 1976).

According to the definition given by Lazarus and Folkman, psychological stress is "a particular relationship between the person and the environment that is appraised by the person as taxing or exceeding his or her resources and endangering his or her well-being" (1984, 19). It is the balance between opposite forces. On one side there is a disruptive event, and on the other end of the balance sits the person's known resources to deal with or to cope with the event. The goal is for the person's resources to restore a feeling of safety and well-being for that person. If the resources are inadequate or not equal to the task or restoration of the feeling of safety and well-being, then the person experiences psychological stress.

In most of the articles on stress, the primary response to a stressor is purported to be the "fight-or-flight" response first described by Cannon (1932). The "fight-or-flight" response is characterized at both the physiological and the behavioral level as the preparation to defend one's territory or flee for one's survival. The biochemical reaction called the neuroendocrine response mechanism, which is set in motion by the exposure to the stressor, is similar in both male and female.

Up to this point, much is the same with males and females. Taylor, Klein, Lewis, Gruenewald, Gurung and Updegraff (2000) claim that at this juncture there is a difference between the actions of the male hormone testosterone and the actions of the female reproductive hormones upon the initiating biochemical, oxytocin. The predominance of previous studies, which led to the "fight-or-flight" theory, was done with males; therefore, the response reported was only that of the male. With the introduction of more research on females, a difference in the response was discovered.

When a stressor or threat is encountered, there is an appraisal or resource assessment phase during which the individual makes a decision on the most appropriate action to address the threat. This may only take seconds but it is in this fleeting time that the crucial response to the stress or threat is determined. During this appraisal phase, females are more prone to establish a relationship with another who is seen as having the power to assist in the midst of a threat to her well-being. This is important because the natural response for females, as described, is to seek another person whom she feels will give her support in addressing the cause of the stress. Because women who are married to pastors often feel alone and/or isolated, this natural response is blocked — the help of another, usually another female, who is seen as capable to assist with the stress is not available. Thus the stress level can be elevated due to restrictions on the natural response for females.

Jochebed states, "My experience has been wonderful at times; challenging at times, and stressful quite a bit." **Naomi** confirms the tendency for women to want to talk to someone: "…sometimes women just want to know that they have someone whom they can talk to." The comments made by **Abigail** noted earlier give support to the premise that the lack of someone to talk to can promote loneliness in women who are married to a pastor:

(She) can be very lonely because she can't share everything with everyone. There are very few people that she can confide in, of any personal thoughts or situations. Sometimes it is a lonely role...not having some female companionship that are just friends, with whom you can feel safe and secure, that whatever you discuss is just between the two of you...you just have to lean and depend on the Lord for everything. I do, anyway—and it seems to work the best.

Although God is the ultimate support, the lack of having another supportive human to whom one can turn to share challenging experiences can cause an increased stress level for these women.

These are some of the issues or concerns observed during the examination of the signs and symptoms of the experience of being a woman married to a pastor. It would be a disservice to leave the process at that point. For there to be healing from the negative conditions found in the experience, some guidance or recommended action must be applied. Just as the women in the study expressed the listed conditions, they also have found ways to respond to those conditions that have been helpful to them. That is the prescription portion—the directions for correction of the condition.

Chapter Four

Prescription

The characteristics exhibited by Priscilla that made her successful during the first century warrant another look in the twenty-first century to see how the women of today can benefit. The women who told their stories of their experiences as women married to pastors revealed that their own ability to be successful in their role showed similarities to some of those same characteristics demonstrated by Priscilla. Looking at Priscilla's responses to life can certainly provide a "mirror for identity" for these women. They, too, in their stories speak of those six characteristics that can serve as a "prescription" for the "diagnosed conditions" encountered.

The first characteristic is that the women indicated you must know who you are as a **person**. The Bible says that God created mankind in His own image, in the likeness of God, with both male and female being included in the term "man" or mankind (Genesis 1:26). Each was an individual, separate and distinct from the other. The psalmist rejoices in the acknowledgement of this creation: "I praise you because I am fearfully and wonderfully made; your works are wonderful" (Psalms 139:14, NIV). Unless you have a firm grasp on who God created you to be, your own gifts and talents and abilities, it is easy to get caught up in the opinions of others. **Abigail** says that being married to a pastor is "nothing I've done or tried to achieve on my own. It's something that He (God) planned out from the beginning of my life as a young woman…Just trying to fit the role that God has, but yet be my own person." She describes further her way to maintain self. "I think just being myself…not putting on any façade…just being real. For some it may be being somebody else…I can't pretend to be anybody else. I have to be me, and what you see is what you get," she chuckles. **Claudia** claims:

People look at a pastor's wife so differently, as if she doesn't enjoy a Tupperware party, Mary Kay, Home Interior, or whatever. (She doesn't get invited) because she might spoil the fun, because she can't talk and be herself, because 'we've got to be careful what we say (when she's around),' not knowing that she's a person, and underneath her skin as a pastor's wife is blood that flows just like theirs, and she loves to have fun and so forth. Sometimes I think they view her as different…not being a person that you can have fun with or not even a person that you can be friends with…they view her as a *role* instead of a *person*.

Hannah discovered that:

Growing through the years and having the support of ministers' wives' groups and the pastor's wife from the church that I came from has given me a different perspective. I realized I couldn't be like someone else. I needed to be myself to be comfortable—for every woman it's different.

Lois states that she is "… just trying to maintain my identity…balancing the needs of the congregation against my needs as an individual, my needs as a mother to my children and also as a wife." **Lydia**

remarks during her interview, "I've been very honest — if it was good or bad, that's who I am, and that's who I've been as a minister's wife."

Persis indicated that she had received much instruction from others on who she should be:

> Early on it was difficult because I didn't know what to do… people *told* me what a pastor's wife should be like, but I couldn't be put into a box like that. So, but now that I've been a pastor's wife for over twenty years, I have my own style, so I like it.

Claudia's comments agree: "First…I had to find out who I was and what God expected of me…to really view how God sees me (as far as my role), then I could really handle it much better."

Julia declares, "I know my role and what I'm to do, and I'm not going to let anybody put me in a box and hinder what I should do." **Huldah** gives this advice about being in "the box": "Don't let them put you in a box…you don't have to be swayed and pulled … (don't) try to be a 'people pleaser.' Be a 'God pleaser.'" **Miriam** relates her experience:

> I learned a long time ago not to worry about what people think." (She laughs.) "I don't have a problem telling people what I can do and what I can't do…whatever I do, I'm going to do the very best that I can.

One woman found that removal from "the box" came with the move to another congregation. "The church I am in now…allows me to be myself, which I like. In my *other* church as a minister's wife, I think they looked to me to play a certain role" (**Dorcas**).

Claudia says:

> There are things that may be thrust upon me…and I sometimes have to step back and see if it is an obligation because of who I am or what I've put on myself, then I try to set some boundaries…I get excited about doing and so I *allow* expectations to be thrust on me. Then I have to go back and see that I brought this on myself…so now I have to find a way of balance.

Damaris also finds she had to reconsider how she responded to the expectations of others:

In the beginning I would just get overwhelmed by all the expectations, but then I had to stop and do a lot of soul-searching and praying. I looked at it, and I said, 'Wait a minute. I answer to God first, then my husband, my family, and then the church.' So after I got my priorities straight and clear, things are beginning to work out a little bit better in that sense.

Some, like **Phoebe,** were comfortable in their own ministries before their husbands became pastors. "I do what I did before my husband became a pastor, and therefore I have a ministry and so does he…I have a role myself," she said. **Dorcas** declared, "Before I met my husband, I had a career. I was secure in myself and in who I was, which is a good footing. It's a good place to be when you know who you are and when you've been saved a long time."

Once you know **who** you are as an individual, you can build a relationship with the Creator who made you because you recognize **whose** you are for you belong to Him. Because of God, the Creator's great love for us, "While we were yet sinners, Christ died for us" (Romans 5:8, NIV). Jesus speaks of the resulting price to fulfill the purpose. "For God so loved the world, that He gave His only begotten Son, that whoever believeth in Him shall not perish, but have everlasting life" (John 3:16, KJV). Our first response to this great love is to have faith and believe in the God who demonstrates it. "(F)or he who comes to God must believe that He is and *that* He is a rewarder of those who seek Him" (Hebrews 11:6, KJV). Priscilla believed and professed her faith in the resurrected Christ. She was a "**professer,**" one who demonstrated the faith she proclaimed and one who later became a **professor,** an instructor and encourager to others in the faith.

These women also **professed** their deep and abiding faith in God. This is the second similar characteristic. Their faith was the primary stabilizing, grounding factor in their lives that caused them to focus and refocus on God's purposes for their lives. **Jochebed** says, "I think my faith has grown stronger…early on in marriage…I had faith, but I did a lot of whining (laughter) and complaining and not understanding… my faith, from then until now, has excelled." According to **Ruth**:

> I would have to say first and foremost that this journey has truly, truly strengthened my relationship in God…through it all I've seen how God has matured me and has grown me, has pruned me and has shaped me and has molded me, and has drawn me so close to Him.

The third characteristic to examine is that of **partner**. Priscilla was a full partner with her husband Aquila both in marriage and in ministry. She was portrayed as important to the marital dyad as well as to the ministry work in which she and Aquila engaged. This work existed even before Paul met them in Corinth for he "found" them when he arrived (Acts 18:2). The women in the study also perceived themselves to be engaged in ministry with their husbands. The degree of engagement varied as did the duties of the engagement but each viewed herself as a participant in the ministry along with the husband. When asked about what she cherishes, **Damaris** answered:

> The part that I play in the ministry with my husband…I see myself as a helpmate. I see myself as an encourager. I see my role becoming more and more distinct and supportive as we're in this together…I know that my presence is valuable to him.

Esther says:

> I cherish the role of being with my husband in ministry and being there to help him and for him to help me in the ministries that I'm with at the church…I know that (God) called him, and I was his wife, then He called me to serve with him.

Phoebe advises, "You have to realize that God has given him (your husband) this ministry. And not only has He given *him* the ministry, you're in the ministry with him." **Huldah** agrees, "I realize that my husband is not his own. He is on a mission, and I'm privileged to walk—work alongside him. Each day brings about new opportunities and challenges to further the kingdom." **Abigail** explains:

> My husband and I are close, and he likes for me to be with him wherever he goes. I think that that's a good thing. It's together-ness for each other but also as a husband and wife to show that marriage is a good thing, that it is a working relationship, that we love each other, not just as pastor and member, but as man and wife—that this is a partnership, that we work together....we work through difficult times in the relationship, problems in the ministry and at home. We share with each other. We work the problems out together.

Claudia says:

> There are times when my husband needs some of my expertise (when interacting with women) because my husband does not al-ways know the motives of women. A woman knows a woman. So I view my role as being a helpmeet, to help steer him when it comes to expectations of women and the boundaries and the balances of ministry.

Although a partnership exists, **Ruth** indicates that the level of involve-ment of the wife in the partnership is individualized based on her abili-ties. "If her husband is called...she's called to be in ministry as well, to whatever degree God has gifted her."

A fourth characteristic to note is that of **producer**. It has been said, "Idle hands are the devil's workshop." Priscilla was far from idle; she was a producer. She was productive in the physical sense by manufac-turing tents, and she was productive in the spiritual sense by providing shelter for Paul and tutoring for Apollos. As the exemplary woman in Proverbs 31, Priscilla was quite industrious.

The twenty women in the study were also producers. The women not only have a time commitment to their church ministry, but most of them also work outside of the home or have retired from working outside of the home. Eleven (55 percent) of the women currently work outside of the home. Another five (25 percent) of the women have retired from work outside the home for a total of sixteen of the twenty women (80 percent) who know what it is like to juggle job and home demands. Some of the positions held outside the home are executive secretary, insurance adjuster, information technician specialist, registered nurse, customer service supervisor, contract director for the military, and teacher's aide. The majority have contributed to the home and to the ministry partnership while functioning in the workplace. The four women (20 percent) who were not in the workplace labor at home and in the place of ministry. In all cases the women voiced that they had produced a positive effect in their chosen worksite. "I used to do daycare...I think people respected me from my daycare...just being visible and supportive to my husband," claims **Jehosheba**. **Persis** described her view of the modern woman who is married to a pastor:

> Nowadays...she needs to be out there helping the ministry (even though) she might work outside of the home full time and have her own career...she actually is part of the ministry.

"I have a full time job so there are some things that I can't do", says **Phoebe**. However, she still managed to teach Wednesday night Bible class for children, teach a Sunday school class, and play the piano for the choir. **Julia** finds that what she learned at her job as a management analyst now proves beneficial. "I don't play the piano, and I don't sing, but I do have good administrative skills that I use to help my husband." She also states that due to her employment, "I put my husband through school." These women were producers in all three spheres: home, ministry and workplace.

The fifth characteristic is to be **pliant**. To be such effective producers, the women married to pastors also had to be flexible and able to adapt to function in an environment of change. When most of the women married, their husbands were not pastors. Not only were some of the husbands not pastors, some were not preachers, and some were not living a Christian life. This highlights another assumption about the experience of women who are married to pastors—that the ministry couple has been at the current level of ministry "all their little life" as one songwriter says. **Jehosheba** says that her husband "had a very successful career in the military." She felt that although the community "respected us from what he did in the military," the church did not. Therefore, when their career moved from the military to the church, she had to navigate the transition from a broad community focus to a differing congregation focus. **Abigail** shared, "My husband was not a preacher when I married him." According to **Damaris** her husband's call to the ministry was unexpected because it came "after our lifestyle and all had been set, and our careers were going another direction, but the Lord said, 'Nope, nope. You're going *this* way.' It just threw me off." But she adds, "Over the years, we learned to adjust. We learned to adapt to whatever the schedule. So in the end, it works out."

Through it all the women stayed the course—they **persevered**. This is the sixth characteristic. The women speak of the growing process that occurred because they remained steadfast where God placed them; they were there for the "long haul." As a result the women spoke of a level of maturity that can only come from the perseverance through the ups and downs of their experiences. Romans 5:3-4 (NIV) states, "Not only so, but we also glory in our sufferings, because we know that suffering produces perseverance; perseverance, character; and character, hope."

Claudia tells her story that embodies the process of perseverance that developed character, which, carried by hope, was able to reap rewards.

> (My husband) decided to go to school, so he resigned his job. And I just loved him enough to follow him. He was working in the bread store…that was the only job he could get, when a lady came into the store. He told her that he was a student at the university. She said, 'Oh yeah…and you're working *here*?' He said, 'Oh yes, you know, you have to support your family.' She kept on getting her

bread, and she said, 'Young man, you're eating the crumbs now, but the slices will come later.' We're enjoying some slices now… Because when you do what God says do, then God's going to do what He is going to do. You just wait on God. I have to tell these young women, 'I cannot tell you it's going to be easy and life is going to be wonderful, but we're eating some slices.' Those were crumbs then, but we're eating some slices now — it's not the money, it's the slices of ministry and the slices of family, the slices of the fact that my husband still has his integrity, the slices that we still have love in our marriage, the slices that our ministries can still go on. Even in the midst of persecution at its best, the kind Paul talks about. What can I say? The scripture says if you are going to live for the Lord, you're going to suffer. But it's better to be righteous than to be right. So you don't seek to be right…but when you're righteous, it carries you for a lifetime. And that's what we seek to do. So if we struggled and suffered a little bit, it hasn't killed us. I think it's made me stronger. I'm a much better person, and God has blessed.

These women were stalwart in their commitment to growing in God's grace through recognizing their *personhood* and becoming a *professing professor* as they served as *partner* in ministry to their husbands. As such the women were *productive* and *pliant* as they *persevered* through life situations and circumstances. Their experiences are not in vain. They want to share what they have learned with other women to help them bloom and be effective wherever God has placed them. The next section is comprised of these lessons learned.

CHAPTER FIVE

Lessons Learned: Shared Wisdom

Proverbs 1:2–5 (NIV) says, "…for attaining wisdom and discipline; for understanding words of insight; for acquiring a disciplined and prudent life, doing what is right and just and fair; for giving prudence to the simple, knowledge and discretion to the young—let the wise listen and add to their learning, and let the discerning get guidance—." As the proverb indicates, women who are married to or plan to be married to a preacher or a pastor would do well to seek wisdom from those who have lived the experience.

Otto, in her book *Between Women of God*, states:

The wealth of spiritual knowledge and down-to-earth wisdom to be learned from women who have walked through the experiences of life is being lost at a time when, more than ever, young women need someone to come alongside them" (1995, 15).

The women in the study have such knowledge and words of wisdom to share with all who will take heed. These words are not meant to be directives to be followed step by step by every woman. They are to serve for reading; ruminating; reflecting; and, through prayerful review, selecting what is applicable to the individual woman for the enhancement of her relationship with God, her husband, family, and fellow creations.

The women were excited to be able to share wisdom with others. **Abigail** says, "I would welcome her to the role that's going to change her life." She says that seasoned women should "just be honest with (those new to the role). Just know it will be a very happy time as well as sad. Don't be surprised that people disappoint." **Eunice** advises, "Buckle up your bootstraps, batten down the hatches, and get ready for a ride!" **Claudia** states:

> I have had a lot of experiences (and that if the account was written) maybe it would help some others. So maybe that's what we need to do. Because these young people, if they don't want to listen, maybe they'll read. Put it in paperback. Somehow or the other, we'll have to get it to them.

She truly wishes that "we could mentor these younger women."

Have a Strong Relationship with God

The first and by far the most important recommendation coming from the women who are married to pastors is to have a strong relationship with God, particularly through prayer. **Miriam** states, "First, I would tell them to pray. Because sometimes we have problems that *nobody* can help us with but God." **Damaris** declares, "I would tell her to first of all pray." **Eunice** says, "Don't forget that God has called you to be a child of God *first*…Keep your communication with Him, your prayer life with Him, strong; remain faithful to Him." **Jochebed** agrees, "The number one thing is that she has to have a prayer life." **Naomi** says, "Pray! Build yourself a prayer life that is consistent." **Persis** concurs, "…just pray, trust God, and He's going to meet you wherever you have to go…Pray, God will take care of you." **Jehosheba** says, "…focus on your relationship with the Lord. That's what you've got to put all your energy and time into…you do have to be selfish with your time with God…Your relationship with the Lord is the only thing that's going to sustain you." **Dorcas** advises, "Have a *strong* prayer life." **Hannah** says:

> Most important is her relationship with God. Study God's word because that's the main thing. It's the *only* thing that is going to help you…That's the main thing — getting a closer relationship with God so that you feel better about yourself and you value yourself.

Ruth admonishes:

> (The closer relationship with God will enable you to) be very sensitive to the voice of God and how the Lord is leading *you*…allow God to use you. Allow God to minister *to* you as well as minister *through* you…Whatever your struggle, whatever your hurt, whatever your pain, yield it to God.

Be the Woman God Created You to Be

The category that ranked next in advice responses is a caution directly related to the issue of personhood — that of the woman recognizing who she is in Christ and being confident and comfortable in becoming that person. You must be the woman that God created you to be. **Lois** advises:

> Secondly, do not lose your identity… Do not make so much change that it becomes fake to your identity even if the changes are good… be real, be authentic, and maintain your own personal identity and integrity in your identity. However, always be ready to grow

into the servant God wants you to be, but don't confuse superficial changes with God's call for transformation and growth.

Claudia wants the woman to:

Be yourself. My grandmother said, 'Start out like you can hold out.' Come into this new relationship the way that you think you can hold out... as time permits, you're going to have to continue it. So don't come into it with any kind of façade because you're going to have to keep that face on all the time. One day they're going to find you, and you won't have that face on. So you need to be who you are.

Deborah says:

Realize that the Lord gave you a personality and spiritual gifts to use in the Body, and be guided by that, and don't try to succumb to pressure to become somebody that the Lord didn't make you. Don't try to emulate somebody else. Be the person God made you to be. Use the gifts He gave you and don't covet or try to develop gifts he hasn't already given you.

Huldah advises, "Be your best person; be your best you." **Julia** says, "I would tell her to just be herself." **Jehosheba** tells the women, "...*know who you are in Christ*... you have to know who you are in Christ and what God has called *you* to do." **Ruth** gives this advice:

Be yourself....Be who you are, and be comfortable in what God has gifted you with, and allow God to mature you in those areas...do not rush yourself and do not allow others to rush you into doing something before you're ready...be genuine...be confident.

Rhoda agrees, "Just be yourself, they'll appreciate that." **Phoebe** says: "Be yourself. Don't try to be something somebody else wants you to be. Be what God wants you to be."

Zora Neal Hurston, in her book *Their Eyes Were Watching God,* tells of Janie, a woman who returns home after a life full of events, some simply wonderful and some terribly tragic. Janie describes her life using opposite terms, very much like the women in the study. It may not be a coincidence that one of the experiences of her life was that of being married to a pastor — the second of her three husbands. Janie, in a lament to her dying husband, says, "But you wasn't satisfied wid me de way Ah was. Naw! Mah own mind had tuh be squeezed and crowded out tuh make room for you in me" (1937/1998, 86). Speaking to this danger, **Claudia** has a word for the husbands: "I would like to say that (husbands) need to let their wives breathe a little bit, *and to be a person — not a puppet, but a person.*"

Be There for Your Husband and Family

The next advice category has to do with the relationship with the husband and family. **Dorcas** states:

Next to having a relationship with Jesus Christ, [the relationship with the husband] comes right second — absolutely second. Because if he doesn't nurture her, she doesn't have anything to give to anybody else — if she's not confident and secure in his love.

Hannah says that the woman should:

…be there to support her husband, let the people see that she supports her husband…to go with him when he preaches out. I think it does make a difference when you're there. Be there on Sunday. There are many, many wives I know that don't even go to church every Sunday, and I think that's very sad because it's very crucial for you to be there.

Naomi warns, "Be there for your husband…always show people that you've got your man's back. It's important for people to see that you and your husband are one…people are watching." **Phoebe** says:

Always be encouraging to your husband…Take out time for your family, and take out time for your husband.…Learn how to balance your church life and your work life and your home life…It's very difficult…it's even harder with someone who has small children…

Be close to your husband and help him a lot…when he comes home, you should be the one to be the nourishment for him.

Abigail instructs, "(She should) develop a personal time with him and for herself, without children, to keep that bond — because (ministry) consumes…you've got to love God and love Him." **Eunice** declares:

Make your home a castle for him, keeping the peace at home, not letting children get out of control, not letting your lives get out of control.…His only constant is you, your home, and your children… make sure that you maintain that constant for him, so you won't lose that love. So you won't lose that zeal for one another, because that's where a lot of messiness comes in.

She cautioned women not to get lost in their own ministry and "forget you've still got to be a wife…you've got to let (him) know *you're* important as well as letting him know that *he's* important.

Jehosheba says women should "Work on their relationships with their spouses." **Jochebed** says, "She should be supportive of her husband…Take care of her husband and take care of her family." "Make sure her husband is taken care of in *every* aspect," she added with a wink. **Lois** comments, "(They) need to laugh and have fun together. It helps them grow and mature together."

The children are not forgotten in the area of advice. The author Heatherly says, "We do not allow pastors' children to grow, to develop; we make no allowances for their immature humanity" (1994, 65). **Abigail** expressed her concern:

Some have that already-built-in notion that our children are bad, because they have that concept that these children are to be saints. But they're just like their children, too…just be the homemaker, wife, and mother, and direct those children in the Lord.

Choose Positive Friendships

Another category of advice deemed important by the women was the problem of friendship. As was addressed in an earlier chapter, women have an innate tendency to seek out another person, usually another female, with whom to interact for the relief of stress. This is known as affiliation. Most women have a need to talk.

A central theme in women's friendships is talking and self-disclosure. Even in early childhood, girls talk and share stories with one another, whereas boys are more likely to spend their time together in active play (Lips 2003, 200). According to Helm and Murphy:

> Women gain actual energy from having a good conversation with a close friend; they feel more empowered to take constructive action in their lives; they gain clarity into their emotions by talking together about fear, guilt, anger and other complex feeling ; and they often gain heightened sense of self-esteem from feeling confident that someone else thinks they're worth listening to (2001, 133).

Most females process things by talking them through. That is why it often drives men to distraction when women talk so much. They think women want them to do something about what they are saying when women really just want them to listen and give them encouragement as they work through their dilemma. When women talk with other women, there is an understanding of this process without frustration or the need for explanation.

Often women suffer in silence, too ashamed to talk with anyone because the woman may think no one else has this problem or that she or her husband will be thought ill of if anyone became aware of the concern. This can be a demonic device used to keep women from tapping into the strength and encouragement that can come from safe and proper sharing with the appropriate person. As a confidante and prayer partner, this person can help you by being a sounding board for listening and a source of biblical and prayerful counsel.

Hebrews 10: 24 (NIV) says:

Let us consider how we may spur one another on toward love and good deeds. Let us not give up meeting together, as some are in the habit of doing, but let us encourage one another — and all the more as you see the Day approaching.

Someone has said that you confess up-line to someone wiser and stronger in the faith (affiliation), and you minister to others down-line to those less strong. That can be situational and seasonal. Sometimes we can be the one being ministered to, and other times we are the ones doing the ministering.

There are two very familiar biblical accounts that reflect an affiliation relationship between women. In the Old Testament we see this occurring between Naomi and her daughter-in-law, Ruth. After the death of her son, Naomi released Ruth to return to her own family but she refused to abandon Naomi, making the well-known declaration of fidelity in Ruth 1:16 (NIV): "Where you go I will go, and where you stay I will stay. Your people will be my people and your God my God." This heartfelt pledge led to the mentoring dyad which would place Ruth in the genealogy of Jesus Christ — all because she listened to the wise counsel of a trustworthy godly woman.

In the New Testament, Mary, who had just been informed by the angel Gabriel that she would be the portal through which God had chosen to introduce His Son in human form, sought comforting counsel with her older female relative Elizabeth (Luke 1:26–45). Elizabeth was also expecting a birth that had also been announced by the angel Gabriel (Luke 1:11–13). This meeting between women also gave rise to another memorable scripture known as the "Magnificat" (Luke 1:46–55). It is interesting to note that *both* Ruth and Mary, who have displayed the affiliation behavior of seeking a mentoring/confidante relationship with another woman, were in the earthly genealogy of Jesus Christ.

Helm and Murphy note that "women friends are central in women's lives" however there is a downside to these relationships. "Because of women's tendency to bond by sharing intimate details of their lives, they may feel more vulnerable when they have a falling out" (2001, 124). As with any action that has sensitive and potentially damaging consequences, one should be very careful when electing another to this very important role of close friend or confidante and should *always* be guided by the Holy Spirit when allowing someone to fill this role.

Colin Powell, the sixty-fifth United States Secretary of State (2001–2005) and former Chairman of the Joint Chiefs of Staff (1989–1993) is credited with several quotes that are applicable when considering the matter of making your choice of friends:

- Never receive counsel from unproductive people.
- Never discuss your problems with someone incapable of contributing to the solution, because those who never succeed themselves are always first to tell you how.
- Not everyone has a right to speak into your life.
- Your friends will stretch your vision or choke your dream.
- Those that don't increase you will eventually decrease you.
- The simple but true fact of life is that you become like those with whom you closely associate — for the good and for the bad.

These are not original thoughts. The Bible, written centuries prior, has already given us instructions on the necessity for caution when choosing friends.

- One who has unreliable friends soon comes to ruin, but there is a friend who sticks closer than a brother. (Proverbs 18:24, NASB)
- Perfume and incense bring joy to the heart, and the pleasantness of a friend springs from their earnest counsel. (Proverbs 27:9, NIV)
- The righteous choose their friends carefully, but the way of the wicked leads them astray. (Proverbs 12:26, NKJV)
- Do not make friends with a hot-tempered person, do not associate with one easily angered, or you may learn their ways and get yourself ensnared. (Proverbs 22:24, NIV)

Seek a Trusted Friend or Mentor

The women in the study also perceive the importance of having a trusted friend, advisor or mentor. "Look for a mentor....Of course we look to God, but that human part of us, that human experience part of it—I think that it would be a good thing to do," advises **Lois**. **Deborah** observes:

> I think a lot of (the women) are going through the motions and re-senting it...They're frustrated, and they're looking for somebody to tell them how to deal with it...find or associate with a pastor and wife in their community, who, in their eyes, seem to have bal-ance and a healthy relationship. I know a lot of these women are suffering.

Thoughtfully, with a tone of sadness, **Abigail** commented:

> She can't share everything with everyone. There are very few peo-ple that she can confide any personal thoughts or situations...some female companionship that's just friends, that you can feel safe and secure, that whatever you discuss is just that—safe. You just have to lean and depend on the Lord for everything.

Several of the women encourage other women to prayerfully seek such a person or group. **Damaris** says:

> Find or pray for a mentor, someone older that she can talk to, and someone she can trust...There are going to be times when she feels lonely and nobody understands her...But I would encourage her to become a part of a support group for pastors' wives, or if there is another pastor's wife to maybe mentor her— an older, experienced woman in the role to help her, that she could talk to and get counsel from.

Hannah agrees to the recommendation but has a further suggestion:

> I would tell her first of all to make sure that she has a mentor of another pastor's wife who's been a pastor's wife for a good number of years. Someone whom she can go to with questions and concerns

about what to do, like how she would handle certain situations. Then, of course, she can have a good friend who maybe is *not* a pastor's wife or a minister's wife. But she cannot talk to her about the congregation or about her husband. Maybe (that friend would be) an out for going to a play or going shopping, or just something other than church so she can keep a good balance.

Miriam adds:

I would tell her to join an organization that can help her. If she is in a place where there are no organizations, then I would say, find a mentor. I believe that mentoring is very helpful. And I believe, even if she's in a city and the mentor that she chooses is in another place, she can still call.

Ruth shares:

You have to have that confidante that you know is going to be very sincere about keeping things to themselves…Be very discerning — be *very* discerning. Don't feel so free that you can share your business with anybody…certainly, *certainly*, develop a relationship with a confidante — preferably an older woman. Definitely establish a spiritual relationship with somebody that is an awesome prayer warrior…somebody that is going to pray on your behalf…You want somebody to tell you when you are wrong that you're wrong.

However some of the women take a very negative view of the confidante being a part of the congregation if the husband is the pastor. **Esther** explains her stance:

I would say *don't* have closest friends in church, that would not be a good idea. When you have close friends, you tell them things; close friends know what you do, when you do it and how you do it… They may have all the intentions of being a closest friend, but then when your husband makes a decision that is not in their favor, they act human. They have all of your closest information, and you can be hurt by that. So although you can have friends, I don't think that it should be your *closest* friend or confidante, but you can certainly have friends in the church. I have plenty of friends in the church, but I don't have that *closest* friend in the church. I would say that if you needed to talk to someone about your relationship with your husband that you be very careful because sometimes the only one you can tell is God and to pray about that situation.

Dorcas agrees:

Have a person who is a praying person that you can trust to be quiet, a person that you can go to that has proven themselves wise in the Lord and a giver of wise, godly advice. Probably somebody that's *not* in your church....I think you need somebody to confide in that's not looking at your husband as the leader, because he's a man just like everybody else, and you don't want them to have any negative thoughts toward him because of you....I don't think people in the congregation should be privy to some of the things you might want to share with somebody....I think it's best if (the person) is somebody who is disconnected (from the congregation).

Rhoda also expressed concern about having a confidante in the congregation:

The most difficult part for me is not being able to find a best friend in the congregation...I find that I have to do that outside of my congregation. ...actually I've become lonesome... it's just a desire that I have, but I know that I can't because it is best that I don't. I know that it would not be in my husband's best interest or mine. I would not want to reveal anything, in the heat of anger, which would mar their image of their pastor.

Phoebe, who has a "good friend" at work that she can talk to but who is not part of her congregation, had a similar warning:

If you need someone to talk to, don't talk to someone that's in your congregation. It's better to talk to an outsider...instead of someone that is in the congregation. It's good if you can talk to someone who is *not* in the congregation — somebody you can trust.

Julia explains, "All of my friends are ministers' wives. There are three of us that are real close...You can't talk to everybody. You can't talk to the people in the church. They'll have your business all over town." **Naomi** advises, "You don't have somebody in church, because heaven forbid you tell your business to just one person—it would be all over!"

It is not that the women discourage a relationship with the congregation or other people they serve in ministry; on the contrary, they truly feel that they must reflect God's love and care toward others. This is basic to the Christian doctrinal tenant, "Thou shalt love thy neighbour as thyself" (Matthew 22:29-30, KJV). This leads to the next area of counsel: how to treat your congregation, ministry members or others outside of your family.

Show Loving Kindness to Others

Lois shared the advice she received:

My uncle, who had been a pastor for years in a Methodist Church said, 'Learn to love the people. If you love the people, they are going to be more in line with following the leadership. If you just love people, they'll know it. You don't have to *agree with them*, but you do have to have a love for them.'

Abigail shared her thoughts:

Don't be surprised that people disappoint. Even some of the ones that you will look up to, at times, will disappoint. I would try to lay the groundwork for you to realize that we are all humans, we all fall short. You'll find out for yourself. People try to sway you up front and tell you certain things about this person and that person. So you go in with false thoughts about people because you don't know and you use those thoughts on which to base your opinions when they are unfounded. And sometimes people just have a dislike for someone else and they have biased you. So don't allow that to be part of your thinking because some people will tell you about everybody and then run—and have you questioning when you should just get to know the person and then go from there. Sometimes those people just need a good friend to talk to, to open up to, and they don't have that, and these other people don't know what they're talking about. Church hurts are bad. I think they're worse than any hurt, and you just have to have a tough skin to go into ministry.

Huldah admonishes women whose husbands were pastors or ministry leaders:

Do not go around trying to do his job. Don't be found guilty of being a little busy body in the congregation. You're over here and stirring up something. You're over there and stirring up something. I think that falls under the category of "zip your lip." Your husband has this tremendous job of preaching the word of God and he's trying to bring sinners to the reality of a saving grace. He's preaching hard and teaching hard, and as fast as they come in, you are sending them out the door with your ugly attitude. You can talk *too* much. Be careful whom you talk to and how much of the family business that you are putting out there. They don't need to know everything about you and your husband. Some women come to the church to air out all their dirty linen—at the church. This is a time for worshipping God! Another thing…don't let anyone take up all of your time. Don't be accused of having your little special clique. Be kind to *all* of the people.

Miriam agrees with Huldah:

Another thing you have to do is not be partial to people. In other words you have to treat all of your members the same. Sure, there's going to be people that you probably like more than others; but in a congregation you can't prefer one over another. You have to treat everybody the same; be nice to everybody, even when you know they're not nice to you—you still have to be nice to them. And that's hard for some people to do. But when you take the face away and just deal with your people, then it's a little easier, because there *are* people in your congregation that are actually unlovable. But you have to love them anyway.

When asked to explain the phrase "take the face away," **Miriam** replied:

In other words don't concentrate so much on that this is Ms. Jones. She's just a member of my church, and she's a member of my church family. I have to treat people like Christ wants me to treat them. Don't think so much about this being Ms. Jones who did so and so to me, but just regard them as a member of the church family, and don't put so much importance on names.

Miriam has more to say to help novices:

The biggest thing that I tell them is not to worry about what people say. You can drive yourself crazy worrying about what people *say* and what people *think* about you. They have a right to think. They can think anything they want to just like you can. So why would you get upset about what people think about you and what people even *say* about you — as long as you know what's right and what's wrong. If you haven't done anything, don't worry about it, because a lot of times people say things just to get you talking so they can find out something. Another bit of advice I tell them is just don't *be* a gossip. Don't *listen* to gossip.

Ruth offers her warning concerning gossip:

Be very careful of those who bring gossip to you. Don't allow members to bring their issues or their problems they have with your husband to you. If there's a member who is upset with my husband about an issue or something that is taking place between them, I immediately cut the conversation…"If you have a problem or a disagreement with Pastor, then you need to take that problem and disagreement to him." It's very easy to get tangled up into mess with church folk. You have some that feud against others, and you have some that disagree with others, and it's very easy to find yourself consumed in that. You have to understand that your relationship with members has to be clearly defined.

Finally, on entering a new venue, **Julia** says:

The best advice that I would give a new pastor's wife is to first observe when going into a church. Learn the people. Learn who's tied to whom. You learn by sitting and observing — sit and observe the people and you'll learn a lot — so that you will know *when* to say and what *not* to say, and be very, very careful of *what* you say.

Phoebe has a similar directive: "When you're coming in, learn the people. As the Book says, 'watch as well as pray.'"

Protect Your Children from Negativity

Another area of concern was that of the protection of the children from any negative consequences deriving from time devoted to the ministry or from people to whom the ministry was devoted. **Phoebe** says:

If the family has children, I think a lot of times parishioners like to put (the pastor's) children on a pedestal, and mothers — parents — need to realize that their children are just like everybody else's children...Everybody thinks the pastor's children should never be able to do what the other children do. They're children, too.

Persis had a similar concern:

Folks ask, 'Your kids go to parties?' Yes. They're kids, so they go to kids' parties, and I'm not going to make them have to stay at home because they're the preacher's kids — I'm not going to do that to them. So they play basketball; they're part of the community. And *you're* not going to make them feel like because they're the pastor's kids — they can't do that.

Lois relates her desire for her children:

It was a little challenging for (the children) in the beginning, and I was protecting them then. I wanted them to have a normal Christian life as teens because for me with my church it has always been good memories. I want my kids to have that, and I believe they have that now that they are adults and married and have children of their own.

The women had much to say to help other women coming along the path over which they are currently traveling. The compassion felt by the women in the study is heard in their words of encouragement intended to make the journey for other women a smoother one.

CHAPTER SIX

Role Adaptability: Shoes that Fit

One of the messages that is heard throughout the narrative from the women is the need to adjust to circumstances and situations arising from being married to a pastor. An innovative typology or classification according to types was composed by E. Robins and J. Kamens (personal communication, June 26, 2009). This typology is presented so that it may assist in the understanding of the responses of the women to the overall role of being women married to pastors. The typology, which describes the adaptability of the women to their role of being married to pastors, was divided into six categories that address the women's enactment or fulfillment of and commitment to the role.

Embracers enact the role by meeting all or almost all expectations associated with the role; they are committed to the role and do not object to any of the main requirements of it. They display a highly positive role enactment and positive or highly positive cognition/affect toward the role.

Women who fall into this category are those who fully support the ministry of the husband using their gifts to enhance the work of the pastor. They truly display the two-for-one phenomenon described by Papanek (1973). Many times the women serve in official and unofficial positions in the church, making every effort to fill any needed spot. Sometimes in the quest to move the ministry forward and meet the needs of the people, they may work simultaneously in multiple capacities. The women see the husband's work as their work and are content to do so.

Susan works at the church where her husband is the pastor. She serves as the church secretary and teaches a mid-week Bible class. When a need arose for a director for the Women's Ministry, she gladly took on that responsibility so that her husband could give attention to other pressing matters. She is also available for counseling sessions, for sick visitation when called upon and her culinary skills are enlisted whenever there is a dinner. The home is immaculate at all times, standing ready for members who may wish to drop in for a visit.

Enlightened compromisers carry out most of the role quite well and accept the practical necessity of doing so in a positive manner despite not being fully committed to it, retaining a sense of autonomy; any resentment is relatively minor and transient. They display a positive role enactment and positive cognition/affect toward the role.

Though committed to the ministry of the husband, these women see themselves as individuals having a separate ministry assigned to them by God that is consistent, complimentary and often congruent with that of the husband. Where there are points of conflict in time and duties, they will weigh the benefits and do what is needed for the greater good of all. They, too, are satisfied and confident in their role.

Anna teaches at the local elementary school and is active in the church where her husband is the pastor. Her passion is for children; therefore, she uses her gifts and talents in the area of the Children's Ministry. When asked to lead the Women's Ministry, she kindly declined but readily sought someone who had the skill set necessary for that task. She expects and receives input from the husband in the home but is understanding when the level of participation ebbs and flows. She is effective and finds fulfillment in her role.

Resigned compromisers carry out most of the role adequately. Although they accept the importance of the role and generally do what needs to be done, they are not very satisfied and may feel forced into their role. They display a positive role enactment and neutral or mildly negative cognition/affect toward the role.

Janet was active in her church as a single woman. When the man she married later announced his call to preach and then became a pastor, she was concerned about how this new role would impact her life. She tried to fit into the role of "pastor's wife" as best as she could in carrying out what she perceived as her duties, but at times she found the task overwhelming. She did not feel comfortable in the role and it showed in her limited engagement with the congregation and unenthusiastic participation in ministry.

Defiant compromisers carry out some or many aspects of the role adequately but dislike the role; they may complain about it, act passive-aggressively, and actively resist enacting many aspects of the role, with possible feelings of being trapped. They display a somewhat positive role enactment and negative cognition/affect toward the role.

Patricia was active in the church where her husband served. She directed the choir and worked with the Youth Ministry. Her contribution to the ministry of her husband, which she felt was something she had to do, was often the topic of her conversation. She frequently interjected her frustration with the role in conversations with the congregants. Although she carried out ministry duties, it was clear that to her it was a duty and not a delight.

Independents do very little in the role but have successfully negotiated this accommodation with their husbands. Wives and husbands accept the women's departure from the expected role and possible disapproval from the congregation. They are able to manage this situation without much distress, and they are personally supportive toward their husbands and families. They display a neutral role enactment and neutral cognition/affect toward the role.

Carol and her husband had been active members of their church for several years. When her husband was installed as the pastor of another church in the city, Carol remained at their home church. She was supportive of her husband and would attend the new church on special occasions and events but did not participate in any of the church ministries. Her husband had no problem with the arrangement. He made it known to the new congregation that her role was to be his wife and that she was not obligated to ministry activities at the new church.

Defiant resisters do almost nothing in the role or deliberately flout role expectations; they are very unhappy about the pressure to enact the role and clearly express their displeasure. They display a negative role enactment and negative cognition/affect toward the role.

Hazel and her husband were not Christians when they married. When her husband confessed Christ, she too joined the church. But when he answered his call to enter the preaching ministry, she became resentful due to the change in their lives. She did not support his educational efforts and vocalized her opposition to his taking a position as a pastor. She often refused to participate in church activities no matter how important the event. After a many years of marital strife and conflict, he returned home after morning worship on the Sunday of his pastoral anniversary to find she had packed her belongings and left the ministry and the marriage.

The above list of categories of levels of adaptability to the role can be useful in understanding how a woman may respond. Just because one may be in a particular category at one point in the ministry does not mean that is where she must remain. Several of the women in the study started out as "defiant compromisers" but with maturation became "enlightened compromisers" or even "embracers." Moving forward through the categories indicates growth in Christian faith. The women in the study want to inspire other women to pursue that growth — growth that comes with a deepened relationship with God.

 CHAPTER SEVEN

Forward to the Beginning

So God created humankind in his own image, in the image of
God he created them;
male and female he created them. God blessed them and said to them,
"Be fruitful and multiply, fill the earth and subdue it; and have dominion
over the fish in the sea and over the birds in the sky and over every living
thing that moves upon the earth."
(Genesis 1:27–28, NRSV)

There is neither Jew nor Gentile, neither slave nor free, nor is there male
and female, for you are all one in Christ Jesus. If you belong to Christ,
then you are
Abraham's seed, and heirs according to the promise.
(Galatians 3:28–29, NIV)

*T*hese two scriptures, one from the Old Testament, from the very first book of the Bible, and one from the New Testament, are bookend confirmations of the intended relationship between women and men ordained by God from creation to revelation. As indicated in the Genesis passage, women and men were created as equals. Because He created mankind, male and female, as different beings but equal beings of value, they received the same blessing from God in Genesis 2:28; God blessed them and gave them permission *to* rule and instructed them on *how* they were to rule. They received the same initial blessing to be fruitful by increasing, reproducing, and having more little Adams and Eves. Mankind, together as man and woman, was given the authority over every other thing in existence on earth. They were equal partners in the original state. "Rule over the fish in the sea and the birds in the sky and over every living creature that moves on the ground." They were co-rulers over everything on earth. However, *no mention is made of one ruling over the other!* This was a picture of parity, of equality. Groothuis, in her book *Good News for Women,* defines biblical equality as "the fundamental biblical principle that every human being stands on equal ground before God; there is no group of persons that is inherently more or less worthy than another" (1997, 19). They were to fill the earth with progeny, all created in the image of God, with the same intent; God created mankind, women and men, as creatures to worship and praise Him. He created them to have a relationship with Him and with each other — a relationship that would reflect the love that God has for His created beings, mankind (male and female). God created a perfect world for His perfect creation, mankind (female and male). God desired and orchestrated a perfect relationship with His creation, mankind (male and female). Mankind, (female and male), at the time of creation, were in perfect relationship with each other.

What happened to disrupt the existence of perfect relationships? Sin. It happened in this idyllic Garden of Eden, and sin has been

disrupting relationships ever since. It fractured the relationship between mankind and God, while at the same time, it destroyed the sym-
biotic relationship of mutual appreciation and respect between female
and male. The Bible chronicles the efforts and lengths to which God has
gone to reconcile mankind back to Himself—to return to this original
bond. There was only one solution to remove the sin barrier and rees-
tablish the broken relationship between the Creator and His creation.
That solution is found John 3:16 (NIV): "God so loved the world that
He gave His one and only Son, that whoever believes in Him shall not
perish but have eternal life." The declaration of the solution is also in
1 John 4:9–10 (NIV): "This is how God showed His love among us: He
sent His one and only Son into the world that we might live through
Him. This is love; not that we loved God, but that He loved us and
sent His Son as an atoning sacrifice for our sins." These verses speak
of God's love for us. In 2 Corinthians 5:18–19 (NIV), the reconnecting
of the relationship is explained: "All this is from God, who reconciled
us to Himself through Christ…that God was reconciling the world to
Himself in Christ, not counting men's sins against them."

God loves each one equally, for the Bible says in Galatians 3:28 that
there is "neither Jew nor Greek, slave nor free, male nor female, for
you are all one in Christ Jesus." Paul is emphasizing the equality of
all stations, races, and genders in the body of Christ. Why is this so
important? It is important because society and culture would have us
to believe otherwise. Women often get swallowed up in the dictates of
those who set the rules. Until recently in our society, whether we want
to admit it or not, these rules were set primarily by and for the benefit
of men using a male perspective as primary or as the norm and relegat-
ing females to the position of secondary or the "other." In many societies women are considered inferior, expendable, and of no consequence.
Lest we who live in the United States of America become boastful of
how advanced we are in our view of women, it was not until the nine-
teenth amendment to the United States Constitution was passed by

Congress on June 4, 1919 and ratified on August 18, 1920, that women were granted the right to vote in this country. This was a right that was withheld from women due to the notion that women lacked the rational thought ability required to participate in the governance under which they existed. That was less than one hundred years ago! (Some individual territories and states had granted that right before it was done on a national level. Wyoming was the first territory to pass the first women's suffrage law in 1890 and Colorado was the first state to do so in 1893.)

Women often are portrayed as weaker in the sense of being less capable. Women are delicate in many ways, but they possess an inner strength that is not necessarily manifested in the physical ability. While in some cases having less physical strength, women are equal in other capabilities and capacities when given the same opportunity. Women are not trying to be men—women just want the same respect as an equal creation of God, to have the personal choice to exercise their God-given abilities rather than be hindered or constrained by the placement of unreasonable restrictions by others.

Women are unique beings created as such by God, neither by mistake nor as an afterthought but by intention. Carolyn Custis James (2005), in her book *Lost Women of the Bible,* indicates that we focus too much on the role of women *after* the Fall or entrance of sin. We need to turn our attention to what it was like *before* the Fall, to the *original* plan revealed in Genesis, and use that as our standard or goal. The traditional assertion of "the man shall rule over the women" is a reflection of a fallen paradigm—a view of the marital relationship *after* the Fall. The relationship fell from God's ideal as mutual and equal to one of hierarchy and rank. The relationship between women and men should be based on God's original intention of parity, not the resulting fallen propensity of humans toward superiority and domination over others in relationships.

The biggest support for women is the Bible yet the main instrument used as opposition to women is also the Bible. It is a matter of interpretation. Katherine Bushnell (1855-1946), a remarkable woman who was born in Illinois, dedicated her life to investigating the matter of women in the Bible. She was a medical doctor, a missionary to China and a biblical language scholar who was puzzled by prohibitions placed on women, seemingly based on biblical edicts. Her book, *God's Word to Women*, published in 1921 has some very interesting points as a result of her research of the matter.

Dr. Bushnell states that the three-part object of her book, which is a series of Bible lessons, is: (1) To point out to women the fallacies in the "Scriptural" argument for the supremacy of the male sex; (2) To show the true position of women in the economy of God; (3) To show women their need of knowing the Bible in its original tongues (Hebrew, Greek and Aramaic), in order to better equip themselves to confute these fallacies.

The less than complimentary interpretation of the role of women is often based in the writings of the Apostle Paul. Quintus Septimius Florens Tertullianus (~160-~225 AD), known as Tertullian, was a Christian author during the 2nd and 3rd centuries who lived in Carthage, North Africa. He based his argument against the active participation of women in church matters on those writings. In his *On the Apparel of Women*, Tertullian says that women should:

> ...affect meanness of appearance, walking about as Eve mourning and repentant, in order that by every garb of penitence she might the more fully expiate that which she derives from Eve,--the ignominy, I mean, of the first sin, and the odium (attaching to her as the cause) of human perdition. "In pains and in anxieties dost thou bear (children), woman; and toward thine husband thy inclination, and he lords It over thee." And do you not know that you are (each) an Eve? The sentence of God on this sex of yours lives in this age: the guilt must of necessity live too. You are the devil's gateway: you are the unsealer of

that (forbidden) tree: you are the first deserter of the divine law: you are she who persuaded him whom the devil was not valiant enough to attack. You destroyed so easily God's image, man. On account of your desert--that is, death--even the Son of God had to die (~200, p. 4).

However, Tertullian did not take into account a passage taken from the Apostle Paul that says, "For since death came through a *man*, the resurrection of the dead comes also through a *man*. For as in Adam all die, so in Christ all will be made alive (1 Corinthians 15: 21-22, NIV, emphasis added).

Another prominent and revered Christian authority had an equally dark opinion of women. Martin Luther (1483-1546), the great German leader of the Protestant Reformation during the 16th century, argued that women were *not* created in the image of God based on their hip width and perceived lack of intellect. His view of women was a reflection of the low level of respect for females during the medieval period (Gamble, 2009).

With such esteemed church fathers adopting this particular stance on women, it is no wonder that these negative early concepts continue to permeate the perception of women in many cultures, societies and religions today. It has taken centuries to accomplish the progress that has been made for women (Kristof and WuDunn, 2009).

Although the Apostle Paul is usually the one who is most quoted when one wishes to constrain women to limited and prescribed roles, there is some question as to the true stance of the Apostle Paul on the issue of women. Grace Preedy Barnes (2004) in her article on Paul as a leader supports Bushnell's stance that there is no error in the scripture but only in the interpretation of the scripture, at times due to cultural bias. She states:

The translators of the King James Version, unable to cope with a woman's leadership role in explaining God's truth more accurately to a man, reversed the order and put Aquila's name first. However, in the Greek, and reflected in modern translations, Priscilla's name appears first. This demonstrates that Paul not only was a servant to all but allowed women and men to serve together...Just as Paul empowered men for ministry, so he empowered women (244). [The names of Priscilla and Aquila in the reference text of Acts 18: 26 appear in this order in the original Greek (Aland Greek New Testament, 2010) and in the modern translations (NIV, ESV, ASV, CEB, NRSV, GNB and others).] Barnes agrees that the ability to understand the original biblical language can shed light on the original intent. In other places, the Apostle Paul commended women and their work for the gospel of Jesus Christ (Acts 16: 13-15; Romans 16: 3-5, 12, 15; Colossians 4:15). This, along with the respect and compassion that Jesus showed to women, sends a different message. In many of His encounters (Matthew 9:22; Mark 12: 43; Luke 7:13, 44-50, et al.), Jesus indicated that women were equally valued in His sight. Just as other new concepts had been introduced by Him, He set a new standard for how women should be viewed.

Women are women. Women are not men; men are not women. It is imperative that we appreciate who God has made us because we are who we are for a purpose designed by Him. We first have to surrender our will to the will of God. Once we have surrendered, we must stay on that path God has for us and be directed by the Holy Spirit. That is where and how growth and maturity happens, both in our relationship with God through Christ Jesus by the power of the Holy Spirit and in our relationships with all others with whom we come in contact.

The women in the study have discovered the much misunderstood concept of personal difference while possessing equality in personal value before God. God has created each of us, female and male, to fulfill the purpose for which we were created. Because of His great love for us all (which includes women), Christ has died for us all, (which includes women). To be valued, to be appreciated, to be respected for who each one is as a person with the individual gifts she possesses — these are worthy and reasonable goals, not only for a woman who is married to a pastor but for all women and all people in general.

EPILOGUE:

The Spouses Speak

Through the Years

Dr. Robert Smith, Jr., Professor of Divinity, Beeson Divinity School of Samford University, Birmingham, AL (1997 to present); preaching for 47 years; former pastor for 20 years; married to Wanda Taylor-Smith for 27 years

I used to act like my wife, Wanda, was suprahuman, self-sustaining, and self-perpetuating. But she actually has blood and needs like me and like all human beings. One of my favorite movies is *Driving Miss Daisy*. Miss Daisy, an old Jewish woman, had her chauffeur, Hoke, an old African American man, drive her to the cemetery so that she could place wreaths on some tombstones. At the cemetery Miss Daisy asked Hoke to help her with the wreath distribution. Hoke eventually had to admit that he could not read and therefore would not be able to place the wreaths on the designated tombstones. She made it easy for him. She asked him if he knew the alphabet. He responded that he did. The grave that Miss Daisy wanted the wreath to be placed on bore the name Bauer. She pronounced the name slowly and told him that all he needed to do was look for the first and the last letters of the name — B and R. Hoke asked about the middle letters of the name. She replied that the middle letters did not matter — only the first and last letters of the name Bauer. Hoke was able to find the tombstone on the basis of the first and last letters B and R without giving any consideration to the middle letters A, U, and E.

Although the middle *letters* did not matter in Hoke's situation, the middle *years* do matter — particularly the middle years of marriage. It has been during the middle years that I have learned a great deal about being married to a pastor's wife — mine. For me the early years represented a period of *Ignorance* — it was a time in which I made many mistakes due to a lack of knowledge. I remember purchasing a green matching outfit with a coordinating purse for Wanda for a special occasion during those early years of marriage. To my great surprise and disappointment, she did not like it. Why? I thought that green was one of her favorite colors. To my dismay I discovered that it was one of her least favorite colors. (She was gentle and kind in providing me with this information). Since that time I have never bought her anything in green!

The middle years are a period of *Enlightenment* — it is a time in which my eyes have been opened, and I have learned more about Wanda. I have not repeated many of the mistakes I made in our marriage due to ignorance. Like the Harold Melvin and the Blue Notes song says, "If you don't know me by now, then you'll never, never, never know me." Today I want to know more of her unspoken journey as a woman married to a preacher who has been a pastor and is now a professor. I want to know her inner dialogues and soliloquies that were not verbalized in restaurants and churches. I want to know more of the gray areas in her life where she wrestles with her own humanity even though she loves the ministry of being called to be a pastor's wife.

Wanda purchased a cell phone for me. It has many features: an alarm clock, a camera, games, a calendar, text messaging ability, e-mail capacity, and many others. However, I've only learned to use two of its many, many features — the capability to make and receive calls. After nearly twenty-seven years of being married to her, I feel like I have learned some valuable lessons, and yet there are many lessons that are still unlearned. If I had it to do again, I would still ask her to marry me, and yet there are some things I would choose to do differently.

- I would be more intentional in demonstrating in word and deed that she is not in competition with my ministry in the church and seminary—instead she is my priority (I assumed that she knew this all along). However, my assumptions did not always match my actions in the area of quality of time that I spent with her and the quantity of time that I spent at the church and in the seminary.
- Instead of just working to become all things to all people in order that I might win some to Christ, I would choose to work harder to become all things to my wife (things that she needed) that I might win her. Sometimes after I left the sanctuary in the church and the classroom in the seminary, I went home to her with too little or nothing left to give her.
- I would begin earlier in our marriage to encourage Wanda in the maximizing of her potential and giftedness in the ministry to which God had called her. She is an enormously gifted person. Much of her ministry is not done in the sunlight of the general public, rather it is executed in the shadows of the private sector:
  - Volunteering as a tutor in a public school,
  - Serving on a committee for a historical society in the city of her birth,
  - Counseling abused women in a Christian counseling center,
  - Ministering to the wounded and the worried through cards and notes, and several other areas of ministerial need.

In the past fifteen years, my wife has spoken to women's groups at national, state, and local conventions and conferences. She has finished a Ph.D. and is launching a writing ministry. As I look back over the years, I would choose to be even more encouraging and gracefully challenging to her with the hope that she would believe more in her potential and giftedness.

- I would have been more proactive as a pastor in preventing the approach of leaders in the church who tried to squeeze her into the traditional mode of "the pastor's wife." I grew up in the church watching the pastor's wife excel in public speaking during special days of the church year (e.g. the Annual Women's Day) and direct or serve as the lead vocalist in the church choir. At that time my wife was not a public speaker, and to this day she is not a leading vocalist in the church choir. It feels so good watching her use her God-given giftedness to glorify God and edify humanity. I wish I had been more proactive in shielding her while gently nudging and drawing her with cords of love into the lane of her divinely ordered purpose. She is now doing things in her ministry that I always knew she could do.

- I would choose to be more receptive of living in the midst of the mystery of being married to my wife without trying to always figure out the *un-figure-out-ability* of her personhood. I have come to accept her more as God's gift to me rather than my personal possession. I am not responsible for *demystifying* her as a mystery; I am responsible for loving her unconditionally as a gift from the Giver of every good and perfect gift.

Victor Hugo once stated, "There is nothing more powerful than an idea whose time has come." Wanda's time has come. These years are the best years of my life as a pastor and professor because I have the privilege of sitting in a box seat watching my wife blossom and bloom in the blessedness and the beauty of her own God-given potential and giftedness. In paraphrasing what Apostle Paul said in his letter to his beloved Philippian church, I say regarding my wife: I have learned to greatly cherish the special gift God has given me. I have not learned everything I should have learned, but I have learned to appreciate and love my wife for her personhood above her productivity.

In 1981 Kenny Rogers sang a love song which expresses my learning and my loving of my wife through the years.

Through the Years

Through the years, you've never let me down.
You turned my life around.
The sweetest days I've found, I've found with you…
Through the years, I've never been afraid.
I've loved the life we've made,
And I'm so glad I've stayed right here with you
Through the years.

Through the years, through all the good and bad
I know how much we had.
I've always been so glad to be with you…
Through the years, it's better every day.
You've kissed my tears away.
As long as it's okay, I'll stay with you
Through the years.

Written by Stephen Dorff and Martin Panser © Universal Music Publishing Group

Lessons Along the Journey

Dr. Daven K. Watkins, Senior Pastor of First Baptist Church,
Pleasant Grove, Alabama;
preaching for 22 year; pastoring for 13 years;
married to Jane Ellen Tilford Watkins for 17 years

Throughout the past thirteen years of pastoral ministry there has been more than one person who has approached me to say, "Pastor, I don't envy you for you have the toughest job in the world." I must confess that there have been a few days along the journey when I have believed this statement from loving parishioners, but most of the time I regard my job as a pleasurable blessing not a painful burden. It is a joy to proclaim God's Word, shepherd God's people, and lead individuals to fulfill God's agenda. My job is not the toughest in the world, yet there are times when I am convinced that being a pastor's wife is far more challenging than being a pastor. I want to believe that I have always valued Jane Ellen, my wife, and as the years have gone by that I have learned to treasure her even more deeply. Allow me to share just a couple of lessons I have gleaned from life and ministry alongside Jane Ellen.

First, the pastor's wife is indispensable to the pastor. In many ways, Jane Ellen is more of me than I am of myself. Don't misunderstand me. I am not denying her individuality for certainly the LORD has crafted and bestowed upon her tremendous talents, passions, and dreams that only she can uniquely fulfill but it is no accident that God

81

has placed us together. In the opening chapters of Genesis, the LORD said, "It is not good for man to be alone. I will make a helper suitable for him" (Genesis 2: 18). For God to declare something as "not good" does not mean that the Lord made a mistake. God pauses so that we will not miss the magnitude of the moment. For all of eternity God has existed in community and never in isolation. God has always existed in the sweet holy society of God the Father, God the Son, and God the Holy Spirit. This Trinitarian stamp of community has been placed by God's design upon His crown jewel of creation. Humanity was never designed to live in isolation. Even the person with the gift of singleness must live in community. Too many times, Satan lures us into a life of isolation where we do not cultivate genuine relationships of community. We can be in a crowded room, have 946 friends on Facebook, and write on numerous blogs and still suffer from isolation.

Adam was trying to navigate through this world in isolation and the LORD declared in Genesis 2:18 that it is not good for man to be alone. To prove his point, the LORD paraded all of the created animals in front of Adam. Adam intuitively noticed that nothing had yet been made that could satisfy his desire for companionship. It became apparent to Adam that all of the animals had companions. There were Mr. Tiger and Mrs. Tiger; Mr. Sparrow and Mrs. Sparrow; and Mr. Lobster and Mrs. Lobster but for Adam no "suitable helper" was found. The phrase *suitable helper* is a two-word phrase in both English and Hebrew. The Hebrew word translated as *suitable* means "similar." The word translated *helper* means "aid or support." In other words, Adam discovered nothing in all creation that was similar to him and could help give support to the God-given commandments delivered to humanity. Adam was incomplete for he could not fulfill the God-given task to fill the earth and have dominion over all the earth without the creation of Eve. At every level, Adam could not live without Eve. In a similar way, I cannot live, serve, or minister without Jane Ellen. She is indispensable to me. To say that a wife is a "suitable helper" is *not* to say that she is second-rate, inferior, or insignificant but it does imply that she is indispensable. I have learned that the pastor's wife is indispensable to the pastor.

Second, the pastor's wife helps the pastor to appropriately relate to all women within the congregation. The married pastor is a one-woman man and every member of the congregation and community ought to know that clearly. Most congregations are over fifty percent female; therefore, the pastor must learn to appropriately relate to all women within the crowd regardless of generation. From Jane Ellen I have learned something about what women think and how women think regarding a host of issues. This has made a profound, positive influence upon my serving and preaching to the whole congregation. Because of her influence, I can better understand the concerns of the elderly widow, the demands of the middle-age lady working in corporate America while raising four teenage sons, the stress of the stay-at-home mother with three babies still in diapers, and the graduate-school bound young lady who is aggressively pursuing a career and Mr. Right simultaneously. Jane Ellen helps me to see from a perspective that is not my own and this helps me to be sensitive and understanding in cases when I might otherwise be impatient and curt.

Because I am the husband of Jane Ellen and the father of a daughter and son, I can more vividly apply the advice given to Timothy from Paul in I Timothy 5: 1 where the author writes, "Do not rebuke an older man harshly, but exhort him as if he were your father. Treat younger men as brothers, older women as mothers, and younger women as sisters, with absolute purity." Relationships are critical within the family of God; therefore, as it relates to the women of the congregation, every lady twenty or more years older than me I am to regard with the love and respect I have for my mother. To each lady who is less than twenty years older or younger than me then I regard her with the love I have for my sister and to every young lady more than twenty years younger than me then I treat as compassionately as I regard my own daughter.

Timothy was living in the Ephesian culture of the first century where immorality was literally around every corner; therefore, the pastor gave his son in the ministry the simple advice to treat all women with absolute purity for he knew the damage that any impropriety could cause. Even though we live twenty centuries removed from Timothy's day, this advice is as relevant today as the day it was first penned.

There are many lessons Jane Ellen and I have learned throughout the past thirteen years and I know we have many more valuable lessons to learn in the years to come. I have discovered that she is indispensable to me and she helps me to appropriately relate to all women within the congregation. Borrowing the words of Solomon, I would say of her, "Many women do noble things, but you surpass them all. Charm is deceptive, and beauty is fleeting; but a woman who fears the LORD is to be praised" (Proverbs 31: 29-30, NIV).

Life with Denise

Dr. Timothy George, Dean of Beeson Divinity School of Samford University;
general editor of The Reformation Commentary on Scripture;
preaching for 51 years; former pastor;
married to Denise Wyse George for 43 years

*I*first first met Denise Wyse George almost 44 years ago when we were both just teenagers. Actually, she was just Denise Wyse back then, and I was the summer youth evangelist at her home congregation, Flintstone Baptist Church in North Georgia. Several things about Denise arrested me from the beginning: her striking beauty, her stately poise, and the fact that she owned her own car. But I was even more impressed by the fact that she was a writer. At our first meeting she showed me a copy of a letter she had written to the newspaper on a matter of public interest. Although she was dating the pastor's son, who was my best friend, somehow the wires got crossed and she and I were married on June 7, 1970.

What has it been like to live with Denise Wyse George for these more than four decades? First of all, it has been a lesson in perseverance for both of us. Although we love each other deeply and have shared together many joys and times of marital bliss, there have also been rugged mountains and deep valleys to traverse. Making ends meet has not always been easy. Neither was raising two beautiful but strong-willed children to adulthood. There has been stress in our marriage but the stress has made us stronger and more devoted to one another. At the core of our connection to one another is rock solid commitment. Back then, we said "I do," and we did. For richer, for poorer, in sickness and in health, till death do us part, all that stuff.

As a matter of fact, we are both writers and we have supported one another in our respective callings. But we do not write about the same things, nor do we write in the same way. Denise is a genius with a computer, whereas I have never touched a keyboard. I dictate everything I write, as I am doing these very lines. This means that we have been forced to learn how to respect one another, and give one another sufficient space to do our own work to maximal effect. Only once have we tried to write a book together, and that experiment nearly destroyed our marriage! Still, I am so proud of Denise's accomplishments and rejoice in the many thousands of lives who have been deeply touched by her work.

At the heart of our life together is a common commitment to Jesus Christ and to the life of faith. Denise's maternal grandparents, Rev. and Mrs. George Williams, were two of the most influential people in my life as well. They taught us the importance of prayer, of reaching out to those in need, and of bringing up our children in the nurture and admonition of the Lord. When our faith has faltered, we think of them and renew our covenant with God. Other friends have also helped us along our pilgrim way, like Rev. and Mrs. Edward Milley, a Methodist pastor and his wife who "adopted" us during our student days in New England. They demonstrated the love of Christ in ways that Denise and I will never forget. We want to be like the Milleys to our own children and to others whose lives we are blessed to influence. Also, our longtime pastor and lifelong friend, Dr. Charles T. Carter, has been a loyal and steadfast encourager to Denise and me in both our personal lives and our professional work. Paul wrote to the Corinthians, "I deliver to you that which I have also received..." (1 Corinthians 15:1). We have received a lot from those who came before us in the family of faith, and we want to pass it on.

As a daughter, sister, wife, mother, writer, teacher, and woman of faith, Denise Wyse George has been blessed with many gifts which she has shared liberally with others. Perfection is not one of her traits, and even less so one of her husband's! But learning how to love, live, forgive, trust, and to follow Jesus Christ wherever His grace may lead marks the life of this special woman with whom I have lived, devotedly and gratefully, these many years.

The Most Important Person in My Life

Dr. Fred Luter, Jr., Pastor of Franklin Avenue Baptist Church,
New Orleans, Louisiana;
President of the Southern Baptist Convention (2012-14);
preaching for 29 years, pastoring for 26 years;
married to Elizabeth Williams Luter for 32 years

As I reflect on my years in the preaching ministry and as a pastor I shudder to think where I would be without Elizabeth, who has been there with me since I was elected as pastor of Franklin Avenue Baptist Church in New Orleans, Louisiana in October 1986. There are SO MANY things that I have learned from my wife Elizabeth the past twenty-six years that I could literally write an entire book, however at the beginning of the book would be, "how in the world could I do what I do without her!" During the years, my wife has been there for me in several crucial areas.

First of all she prays for me. My wife gets up every morning at 5:00 AM and prays for me, prays for our children, prays for our families, and prays for our church. Recently she suggested that it would be really special if I would get up with her so that we could pray together. Being the "night" person that I am, I told her that "Jesus is not up at 5:00 AM in the morning, therefore I will get up when Jesus gets up, about 8:00 AM!!" But seriously, I have no doubt that a lot of the reasons

I am the man, the husband, the father, and the pastor that I am today is because of the prayers of my wife. As a matter of fact Elizabeth is known throughout the church not only as my wife, but as a prayer warrior.

Second, she encourages me. Every pastor knows that ministry can be very trying at times. There are times when the deacons get devilish, the trustees get tricky, the choir gets cranky, the ushers get ugly, and the members get messy! As a result of the stuff that happens in the ministry, there have been times when I have come home discouraged. However, no matter how bad things may get at church, I always know that once I get home, Elizabeth will have a word of encouragement for me. I wish I could share with each of you the hundreds of hand written notes and cards I have received from her through the years. It is as if God has given her the words I needed at the time to make me feel that "this too shall pass."

Another way that my wife encourages me is when I am preaching. My wife has a way of shaking her head in agreement no matter how bad the sermon may be. Members and guests have often commented how they did not pay a lot of attention to my sermon because they were distracted by watching Elizabeth while I was preaching!

Third, she counsels me. One of the wisest things a pastor can do is to LISTEN to the wise counsel of his wife. Through the years Elizabeth not only has become my best friend, she has also become someone who I know has my best interest in mind. I am by nature a people person. I never meet a stranger. Therefore I am the type of pastor that has a big heart for every member and believes that everyone is always telling the truth. Besides no one would lie to their pastor!! So every once in a while Elizabeth would warn me to "watch out for Brother So-and-So" or "be careful around Sister So-and-So. There is just something about him or her that concerns me." Of course I would then defend Brother So-and-So and do the same for Sister So-and-So, until one day at a church meeting or some other occasion each of them would cross the line in their actions or by their words. Immediately when it happens the thought would come to my mind, "My wife told me to watch out for you!" It was during those times I realized that my wife had the gift of discernment and she is always looking out for my best interest. Therefore I beg and plead with every preacher and pastor to listen to your wife.

And finally, **Elizabeth keeps me humble.** God has truly blessed our ministry at Franklin Avenue through the years. From starting out as a Southern Baptist mission church with fifty members to now the largest Southern Baptist congregation in the state of Louisiana has certainly been a blessing from God! With that kind of success in ministry come invitations to speak at events all over the country. I have had the honor of preaching for numerous revivals, association meetings, state evangelism conferences, college graduations, pastors conferences, as well as make history by being the first African American preacher to preach the annual message at the Southern Baptist Convention in 2001. By God's grace, I again made history on June 19, 2012 when I was elected the first African American President of the Southern Baptist Convention. It is not unusual for me after one of these events to come home and "glow" in the moment. Elizabeth would notice my head getting two to three times its normal size and would bring me back to reality by saying, "Baby, I am so proud of you, now don't forget to put the garbage out tonight!" And once again I enjoy my slice of "humble pie!"

I started this piece off by saying I do not know how some preachers and pastors make it in ministry without their wife; I know for sure I would not be where I am today without Elizabeth. If anyone would look up in a dictionary the term "pastor's wife," I have no doubt you will find a picture of "the love of my life, apple of my eye, my prime rib, and my good thing," Elizabeth. She is a perfect model of what a pastor's wife should be. Besides that, she is the most influential person in my life!

The Hardest Job in the Church

Dr. Michael Duduit, Dean of the College of Christian Studies
at Anderson University, Anderson, SC;
Teaching Pastor at The Bridge, Anderson, SC;
Executive Editor of Preaching *magazine; preaching for 40 years;*
married to Laura Duduit for 26 years

Over many years of service in the church and working with church leaders in a variety of setting, I have come to the conclusion that the hardest and most challenging job in most churches is not the role of pastor or some other staff position. The most challenging role in most churches – particularly smaller ones – is that of the pastor's wife.

About twenty years ago I worked with Jill Briscoe – a ministry wife with a big heart for her fellow ministry wives – in developing a newsletter, then magazine for women married to ministers. My organization published it for some time before giving it to Jill's ministry, and I still recall the heart-breaking letters we would often receive from ministry wives who felt isolated, overlooked, even rejected.

We'd get letters from women married to the pastor of a small church, far from her home and family. She would lament the fact that her pastor-husband was often scurrying to meet unrealistic expectations as the lone staff member of a church – yet the expectations on the wife were equally demanding. The pastor was often paid a pittance of a salary, but the wife was not to work outside the home so that she would be "on call" for needs of the church. She was expected to be a role model of a wife and mother, yet at the same time to be there to teach a class, help with the nursery, play the piano, host the ladies' mission group, make hot dogs for the youth gathering, and on the list went. It was clear from some of the letters we received that many ministry wives were on their last legs, exhausted physically and emotionally, and ready to cast aside husband and church because they just couldn't do it any longer. Tragically, too many congregations do this to their ministry families, then they wonder what went wrong when the pastor and/or his wife crashes and burns.

There are some things we can do – as pastors and ministry wives – to help protect those ministry marriages:

Recognize that your family is a higher priority than your church's activities. God is our first priority, but in the economy of God your family comes second. To paraphrase the saying of Jesus, what does it profit for a man to gain his church but lose his family? Churches can often have unrealistic expectations about pastors and their spouses, and we have to lovingly but firmly teach them that the pastor's marriage is more important than his attendance at every committee meeting.

Churches are like credit cards – they'll let you keep loading up until finally you hit a limit. Young pastors, in particular, often are so anxious to serve, to be needed, to be loved that they let themselves be exploited; taking on any and every assignment someone in the church throws at them. As a result, it's easy for a pastor (or ministry staff member) to spend every waking hour doing church work and coming home with nothing left for family. The same thing can happen with a ministry wife who gets caught up in serving and has nothing left for her husband. Ministry marriages can become ticking time bombs if we neglect them.

And if it comes down to a decision, which would you rather keep: your family or that pastorate? (And trust me, the church that will willingly let you destroy your family will also toss you out on your ear at the first indication that your family is struggling.)

Help your church understand that your family – not only your spouse, but also your children – is a priority that you will protect. Not only will it help your family – it will also be a model that may help save some other marriages in your church and community.

Schedule time for family. One of the ways you spell priority is: TIME. Ministry can easily suck up all the available hours in your day, so it is essential that you schedule your days and weeks so that there is time to invest in your family. Let your calendar be your friend by using it to schedule blocks of time for needed ministry activities, but also for time with your family. Schedule a regular date night with your spouse – don't let the romance seep out of your marriage. Schedule time for the children, whether that's arranging the schedule to attend their games and recitals, or just arranging a Saturday morning time to take them to the bookstore or movie and then lunch together. (If funds are tight, make it a picnic with a homemade sandwich – the memories will be just as good!)

Set boundaries for your church and yourself. Early on in a ministry, it's important to let the church know how much you value your marriage and family and that such a commitment requires setting boundaries. One such boundary the pastor can build to protect his wife is to clearly identify what she will and won't be doing for and at the church. Do it lovingly and with grace, but explain that your wife's first calling is to her husband and family, and that means there are certain things she'll be doing for the church – as would any faithful member – and other things she should not be expected to do. Then protect her when the inevitable effort comes to bust that boundary.

Likewise, there are some behavioral boundaries that pastors and spouses should set for themselves, to protect against even the hint of moral failing. For example, as a pastor I have long set limits on how I relate to other women (apart from my wife and family). I will not drive in a car with another woman alone. I will not travel alone with a member of the opposite sex, nor will I eat out alone with a woman who is not my wife. Has this occasionally caused inconvenience? Yes. Has it also protected me from false accusations and troubling encounters? Absolutely.

I am fortunate to be married to the best wife in the world! Her own commitment to serve Christ and His church is a challenge and encouragement to me. But I am not willing to let her be a casualty of the church. My family and yours are too important. They are God-given treasures, so let's guard them as such.

Pearls of Wisdom

Rev. James Dixon, Jr., Pastor of El-Bethel Baptist Church, Fort Washington, Maryland; preaching for 37 years and pastoring for 34 years; married to Dessie Harris Dixon for 41 years

As a minister of the Gospel for 37 years and a pastor for over 34 years I have seen, heard and felt the pain, the joys and the disappointments of many ministers' wives including Dessie, my own wife of 41 years. My first experience came in the beginning of our ministry when the wives of senior pastors of the church decided to give advice to my wife on how to handle ministry. The advice they shared with her went against most of the principles on which she had based her life but because she held them in such high regard and had a desire to do well, she tried it their way. In a very short time, I watched this woman, who was so nervous and scared but yet feeling blessed about her new role as a minister's wife, soon turn into someone who became depressed, angry and uncertain about what God was calling her to do. She was hurting inside and keeping it to herself because she assumed I would not understand what she was going through; so much so until the pain began to affect her physical health. She had allowed someone else to set the expectations for her life and to change who God had created her to be.

After Dessie finally opened up her heart and shared with me what she was really feeling, her life in ministry began to change. Since that time I have watched her bloom into the wholesome person and child of God I knew she could become. For her to be able to adjust and enjoy serving God through this call did not happen overnight, but I encouraged her faithfully. Over the years I have continued to support, listen and encourage her as she strives to fulfill God's will for her life.

Throughout the many years I have served as a pastor, as well as a denominational worker, I have had many conversations with other wives of preachers who are at a point where the joy of serving God has gotten to be such a struggle. They are tired of having to fight to stay on top because somewhere or somehow this calling has become a burden that they cannot carry on their own. If I could offer a few words of wisdom that I have shared with my wife and many other wives of preachers and pastors who have found themselves in a similar place in their lives it would be this:

- **Live your life in the key of B-Natural:** Let God define who you are so that the real person on the inside will be reflected on the outside. Always be true to yourself so that you can be true to God and others. God knew you before He called you to join Him in this work. He knew everything and yet He chose you anyway. Your significance is found in Him and Him alone. No one has the right to control you as a person or set expectations for you to follow. That is the responsibility of your heavenly Father through the power of the Holy Spirit. Make sure you are prayerful as to your choice of a mentor or example you want to follow because everything that glitters is not pure gold.

- **Know your own identity.** So many wives have lost their identity in their husbands. Even though we are created one with our mates, God created each individual in his or her own uniqueness. When ministers' wives lose their identity in their husbands lives they cease to be who they really are and become who their husbands want them to be. When devastating situations occur in your lives and your mate is gone you still have to live on. If you incarcerate yourself in the other person's world you just may die with him even though you're alive in the flesh. I have witnessed this happening too many times and the wife is totally lost. Please know *who* you are and *whose* you are!

- **Establish your own faith in God and walk in it.** When we first started in ministry my wife trusted in me as I trusted in God. She depended on my faith and not her own. I knew she had a personal relationship with God but she did not know how to put all of her trust in Him. One day her faith was challenged when she encountered a health problem that caused paralysis in her legs. She could not walk at all and was confined to the bed for days. While she was down the Holy Spirit had her full attention. The Lord challenged her to do self-examination of her faith. As she cried out to God for His healing power she fell under conviction because she realized that she was not walking in her own faith but in mine. It was a real defining time in her life and in her relationship with the Master. God answered her prayer and restored her health completely. Our ultimate faith in God can be the determining factor in how we survive the things we encounter in life.

- **Make prayer the centerpiece of your life.** One of the first questions I ask when I counsel with people, pastors and their wives included, is "How is your prayer life?" Most of the time the responses are not very good. Prayer will relieve a lot of the stress in ministry. Pain is real and ministry can bring a lot of stress and pain into our lives and to our families. God created the family before He created the church so family is important to Him. Don't be afraid to spill your guts to the Father. He knows anyway and He wants us to share what we are feeling. If you are angry and disappointed or hurt and feeling abused you are free to tell Him and He is very capable to handle it in love. It is a very liberating experience. His word tells us in 1 Thessalonians 5:17 that we are to "pray without ceasing" and Psalm 50:14-15 says to offer to God "a sacrifice of thanksgiving, and perform your vows to the Most High, and call upon me in the day of trouble; I will deliver you, and you shall glorify me." God will help you through every trial if you are obedient to His word and trust Him without doubt. And let me add that open communication with God will help you to keep open communication with your spouse.

- **Be intentional about living a life of integrity.** Integrity must be the central factor of the soul so that you gain the respect of others as well as respect for yourself. One of the many things I admire about my wife is that she is a woman of honesty. She says what she feels and is very truthful to herself and to others and she does it very tactfully and in love. When a woman is true inside and out, in her private and public life she can stand steadfast and constant on what she believes. She is consistent in her thoughts and is not blown by every wind. Her reputation is spotless and she is one that God can brag on. Her love for Him supersedes anything else in her life for He is her master teacher and she tries to exemplify His character. A woman who is honest with her life can be honest with God and others.

It is my prayer that these words will touch the life of each reader and challenges her to become all that God has ordained her to be. May she walk in His spirit daily and become determined in her mind and heart that nothing will interfere with the commission and call that God has placed on her life. As she serves alongside of her husband, together may they spread the fragrance of Christ as they impact the world and the kingdom. Women of God, I encourage you to enjoy the freedom that God has given unto you.

Roles, Relationships, and Reason: A Brief Statement

Dr. James Earl Massey, Dean Emeritus & Distinguished
Professor-at-Large, Anderson University School of Theology;
Dean Emeritus, the Tuskegee University Chapel;
founding pastor of Metropolitan Church of God, Detroit, MI;
preaching for over 65 years;
married to Gwendolyn Kilpartrick Massey for 61 years

Dr. Wanda Taylor-Smith's book has offered a platform from which women married to preachers and pastors have been speaking. As a long-time husband (over sixty years) whose wife has been at my side during my roles as preacher/pastor/professor/seminary dean, I have learned much about "hermeneutics" and role adaptability by observing my wife's responses as a companion in marriage.

First being both the child and grandchild of pastors, she came into our marriage with a strong respect for the ministry and a healthy view of church life. Having watched the healthy relationship of her preacher-father and mother, and that of her preacher-grandfather and grandmother, she knew that she, too, could relate meaningfully and supportively in our marriage.

Second, she understood, as did I, that both marriage and ministry require natural gifts and spiritual enablement, and that self-growth must forever remain a foundational concern. She recognized my pastoral gifts, and supported me in further training them for use, but she also was aware of her own gifts for service both within the church, and beyond the church setting. Her occupational interests led her to become a nurse and later a professional counselor. As church member, she sang in one of the choirs, taught a Sunday School class, and was a counselor to young adults. As pastor and spouse, we were intentional about supporting each other in our gift-based roles; mindful that all gifts — whether natural or spiritual — contribute to meeting human need, solving problems and aiding possibilities for people. Recognizing, as Paul explained it, that "We have gifts that differ according to the grace given us" (Romans 12: 6), we both sought to "outdo one another in showing honor" (v. 10b) as we served the Lord in our distinct roles.

Third, when invitations came for me to serve in other spheres of ministry (campus minister, denominational radio voice, professor, dean of the university chapel, seminary dean), we shared openly and prayed fervently to discern the wisest course of action — and also to secure a concurrent role for Gwendolyn with every move we agreed to make. We remained on guard against disconnection, satisfied only with our reality, always standing with each other in a simple but steadfast relationship based on loving trust and a trusting love.

What I have written here is a faithful reflection on what Gwendolyn Inez Kilpatrick Massey has contributed to me as a person and to my path as a minister. Free to be herself, and trusted as one who loves God and me, my wife helped me to develop as a person and to better offer leadership in the ways and places entrusted to me. My vocation did not deprive her of her identity and her identity did not depend on any role imposed upon her from without. We have long rejoiced that both marriage and ministry require communal actions, and that both the minister and the minster's spouse succeed best when neither one acts selfishly but remains free to serve and bless on the basis of their own life-enhancing, grace-sustained gifts. This is not only reasonable, it also responsibly honors the trust God placed in us.

Conclusion

There is an African proverb that relates that the hunter will always be the victor until the lion is allowed to tell its story. This book has been an attempt to allow the lionesses, women married to pastors, to tell their stories. Because it is an experience the women have lived, the telling of their stories has powerful credibility.

Janie, in *Their Eyes Were Watching God*, returns home from her journey through a life filled with many ups and downs. As she reminisces about her life to her best friend, Pheoby, with whom she has reconnected, she says, "It's a known fact, Pheoby, you got to *go* there tuh *know* there. Yo' papa and yo' mama and nobody else can't tell yuh and show yuh. Two things everybody's got tuh do fuh theyselves. They got tuh go tuh God, and they got tuh find out about livin' fuh theyselves" (Hurston 1937/1990, 192). These women who are married to pastors have had to find out about living by doing just that—by living. In the process of living, they have gone to God for themselves to find their purpose. As they traveled along their life journeys, they have gained wisdom. The women "know there" because they have "been there." They have been renewed, restored, redirected, and redefined by the love and meaning found in God's plan for their lives. The women in the study had a desire to share the wisdom they have gained along the way so that it might encourage every woman who is married to a pastor in her own personal life's journey. For this we give God praise!

Questions For Discussion

1. How do you view yourself in the role of a woman who is married to a pastor?

2. Is it any different than being married to a man in any other profession or calling? If so,   how? If not, why not?

3. Do you think there are expectations associated with your role as a woman married to a pastor?

    If so, what are these expectations?

    Where do they originate?

    What is most important?

4. How do you respond to the expectations?

5. What parts of the role do you cherish and enjoy?

6. What parts of the role do you find most challenging?

7. What boundaries have you established to protect your marriage and family? How did you establish the boundaries?

8. How do you deal with criticism of you and/or your husband?

9. What are ways that others can support you, your husband, and family as you minister to them?

10. If you could, what would you do differently that would be beneficial now?

11. How can your husband be a greater support?

12. What can you do to encourage other women in the same role? Have you done it?

References

_____*Aland Greek New Testament*. 2010. Fourth Revised Edition in cooperation with the Institute for New Testament Textual Research, Munster-Westphalia. D-Stuttgart, Germany: Deutsche Bibelgesellschaft.

Bachus, Wilma Norman. 2005. *Called to the Ministry of Pastor's Wife*. Nashville: Townsend Press.

Barnes, Grace P. 2004. "The Act of Finishing Well: Paul as Servant Leader" in *Mission in Acts: Ancient Narratives in Contemporary Context*, Robert Gallagher and Paul Hertig, eds. Maryknoll, NY: Orbis Books.

Bushnell, Katherine C. 1921. *God's Word to Women*. Mossville, IL: God's Word to Women Publishers.

Cannon, Walter B. 1932. *The Wisdom of the Body*. New York: Norton.

_____Colin Powell Quotes. http://www.goodreads.com/author/quotes/138507.Colin_Powell. (accessed 2-5-2013).

Custis James, Carolyn. 2005. *Lost Women of the Bible*. Grand Rapids, MI: Zondervan.

Dickens, Charles. 1867/1985. *Great Expectations*. New York: Dodd Publishers.

Gamble, Richard. 2009. *The Whole Counsel of God, Vol. 1.* New Jersey: P&R Publishing.

Gower, Ralph. 1987. *The New Manners and Customs of Bible Times.* Chicago: Moody Press.

Groothuis, Rebecca Merril. 1997. *Good News for Women: A Biblical Picture of Gender Equality.* Grand Rapids: Baker Books.

Hager, W. D. and L. C. Hager. 1996. *Stress and the Woman's Body.* Grand Rapids, MI: Fleming H. Revell.

Heatherley, Joyce Landorf. 1994. *Balcony People.* Austin, TX: Balcony Publishing Company.

Helm, Pat and Susan Murphy with Susan Golant. 2001. *In the Company of Women.* New York: Jeremy P. Tarcher/Putnam.

Hurston, Zora Neale. 1937/1998. *Their Eyes Were Watching God.* New York: Harper Perennial Publishers.

Kristof, Nicholas D. and Sheryl WuDunn. 2009. *Half the Sky: Turning Oppression into Opportunity for Women Worldwide.* New York: Random House, Inc.

Lazarus, R. S., and S. Folkman, S. 1984. *Stress, Appraisal, and Coping.* New York: Springer Publishing Company.

Lips, Hilary M. 2003. *A New Psychology of Women: Gender, Culture, and Ethnicity.* New York: McGraw Hill.

Otto, Donna. 1995. *Between Women of God.* Eugene, OR: Harvest House Publishers.

Papanek, Hanna. 1973. "Men, women, and work: Reflections on the two-person career." *The American Journal of Sociology* 78:852–872.

Randolph, Elizabeth, ed. 1994. *PDR Nurses' Dictionary*. Montale, NJ: Medical Economics.

Sanders, James A. 1976. *Hermeneutics: The Interpreter's Dictionary of the Bible*, supplementary volume. Nashville: Abingdon Press.

Selye, Hans. 1956. *The stress of life*. New York: McGraw-Hill.

Selye, Hans. 1976. *Stress in health and disease*. Boston: Butterworth.

Taylor, M. G., and S. F. Hartley. 1975. "The two-person career: A classic example." *Sociology of Work and Occupations* 2:354–372.

Taylor, Shelley E., Laura C. Klein, Brian P. Lewis, Tara L. Gruenewald, Regan A. R. Gurung, and John A. Updegraff. 2000. "Biobehavioral responses to stress in females: Tend-and befriend, not fight-or-flight." *Psychological Review* 107:411–429.

Tertullian. ~200 AD. *On the Apparel of Women*, Book I. Translated by S. Thelwall. From *Ante-Nicene Fathers*, Vol. 4. Edited by Alexander Roberts, James Donaldson, and A. Cleveland Coxe. Buffalo, NY: Christian Literature Publishing Co., 1885.) Revised and edited for *New Advent* by Kevin Knight.

_____U.S. Bureau of Labor Statistics. http://www.bls.gov/cps/wlf-table24-2011.pdf Annual Social and Economic Supplements, 1971–2010, Current Population Survey, 77
Contribution of wives' earnings to family income, 1970–2009 (accessed 12-30-2012).

_____U. S. Bureau of Labor Statistics. http://www.bls.gov/opub/ted/2012/ted_20120501.htm (accessed 12-30-12).

www.ingramcontent.com/pod-product-compliance
Lightning Source LLC
Chambersburg PA
CBHW060150300526
45790CB00014B/487